REAL TALES OF A MOMPRENEUR:

TRUE STORIES OF BUSINESS, BABIES, BALANCE

Copyright Notice

Real Tales of a Mompreneur:
True Stories of Business, Babies, Balance

Copyright © 2017 Kendra Garcia

All rights reserved, including the right to reproduce this book or portion thereof in any form whatsoever.

This book is designed to provide accurate and authoritative information with regard to the subject matter covered. It is sold with the understanding that there is not a professional consulting engagement. If legal or other expert advice or assistance is required please seek a licensed professional in your area.

For information on bulk orders or to have Kendra Garcia speak at your event, email Lifestrategistkg@kendragarcia.com

Table of Contents:

Page 4	Kendra Garcia - *Real Tales of a Mompreneur*
Page 20	Sabrina Wright – Mompreneurs *Levels of Success*
Page 37	Tye Miles – *PowHer of Perseverance*
Page 58	Lakesha Reed-Curtis MSN, RN– *Just A Girl Who Decided to Chase Hers*
Page 75	Lenise R. Williams, Esq. – *Raising Business & Babies*
Page 89	Arleigh Hatcher – *Heart of a Momprenuer*
Page 109	Toni Robinson – *Mom in Chief*
Page 130	Latanya Sanders-Kelker – *A Journey Worth Taking*
Page 146	Colette Glover-Hannah – *Managing Partnerships, Parenthood & Presentations*
Page 169	Melissa Alexander – *Mommy Means Business*
Page 188	Jennifer Logan – *Turning Dreams Into Reality*
Page 206	Trinese Summerlin – *A Mom By God's Loving Grace*
Page 224	Tiffany Simmons, Esq – *Making the Case for Successful Moms to Be*

Chapter One

Real Tales of a Mompreneur
By: Kendra Garcia

Sitting here at my desk and all I can think about is how awesome God is. Never in my wildest dreams did I, a girl from every hood in Nashville, TN, think that I would be a business owner or successful in my own right.

My struggles started from an early age. Dealing with instability. Moving from place to place. Not knowing if when I got home from school if the lights or the water would be disconnected. Not knowing what the climate would be in my household on any given day. Would there be fighting? Would we have a quiet family night? So many uncertainties that I had to deal with at such a young age that I could not see what my future would look like.

Sure, I have people in my family that have stepped out and experienced entrepreneurial success, but that seemed so far fetched for me. I could not see that for myself because I did not have focus nor any clear goals. My only goal as a high school student was to graduate baby free. My mom made it clear that a teen pregnancy was not going to be tolerated in her house and neither was a high school drop out.

I can clearly remember one day in my job success class being asked what I wanted to be when I grew up. I had to be maybe 15 or 16 at the time. I had no clue, but I knew that I wanted to work at a desk, dress nicely, and type. I had a love for computers and technology but had no clear defined goals. My answer to the question was, "I want to be a secretary". That was my idea of a dream job at that time because I equated the job duties of a secretary to something I wanted to do. I can still remember the look of disappointment on the teacher's face when I said that. She was a young black woman in her mid to late twenties. She saw so much more in me and tried to steer me in a different direction. "Don't you want to do more than be a secretary? What about owning your own business?", she asked. I shook my head "no" and stuck with the first answer I'd given. At that time I did not realize that she was trying to get me to see more and to think outside of the box. However, now at age 35, 5 kids and one husband later, I get it. I've finally stepped outside the box and I'm living a dream I did not know that I had; I am a momprenuer.

    Hi, I'm Kendra Garcia. A Life and Business Coach from Nashville, TN. I have a husband, five kids and no pets. I enjoy reading, singing at the top of my lungs in my car, eating great food, and a good glass of wine. Most importantly I enjoy helping others do something I couldn't do at one time- realize their passion, goals, and dreams and then live them.

    Growing up on both sides of the tracks gave me two different perspectives. I was able to see what both stagnation and growth looked like. The times that my paternal grandmother or aunts would get me and take me to the "good" side of the tracks was when I was able to see progression and growth. Growing up on the "bad" side of the tracks or the hood is where I was able to see what stagnation or being stuck looked like.

I thank God for the times I was able to spend with my grandmother and also my older cousins. If it were not for those moments, I don't think that I would be the woman that I am today. My grandmother raised seven kids and had a hand in the raising of all of her grandchildren even to this day with great-great grands. I have a large family; we could fill a small church. She played a huge role in helping me to see that the world was round and that there was so much to discover.

Growing up my mother and father struggled with drug and alcohol abuse so it was nothing for us to come home to a dark house because the lights were off or to no running water because the water was off. We were used to arguments and fights between our parents. I was a worrying teenager. I worried that the lights would be cut off, I worried that we wouldn't be able to pay the rent and we'd be forced to move. I worried that I wouldn't be able to go to the prom or even pay my senior dues to graduate. I worried that I wouldn't be able to find the money for college and I'd be stuck just like some of the people I witnessed growing up. I just worried all of the time.

My senior year in high school was no different than any other school year. We had family drama. My mom was dealing with some serious issues after the untimely death of her older brother and she was in rehab at the start of my senior year. That year started off rough but finished strong. I had to take care of my younger siblings. Due to my diligence to get and keep good grades, my senior schedule was very light and I was able to leave campus early. The early dismissal allowed me to work extra hours at my job to save money for the things I needed my senior year. That year was tough, but I grew a lot. I got into the college of my choice, Austin Peay State University in Clarksville, TN. It was only 30 minutes away from home.

The day of my high school graduation my family did something that changed my life forever. At that time my older cousin was working in London, England. Together my family contributed money and they paid for me to spend the summer before college in London. I was so incredibly happy, yet nervous at the same time. Outside of Tennessee I had only traveled to Georgia and Kentucky and never for more than two days. This would be my first international trip and my first extended trip away from home. That trip changed my life. It gave me a new perspective and set me on a path of going after I wanted no matter what, even though at the time I did not know what I wanted.

I went to college with a bright outlook on life because of my experiences from my trip. Because of my love for Oprah Winfrey, I decided to major in Mass Communications/radio and television broadcasting. I was truly happy and for the first time I was worry free. I was not stressed about my parents fighting in the home or electricity being disconnected- I was free. I also did not stress about how I was going to pay for school as I had a scholarship, grants and other funding that covered my expenses. I was ready to take college life by storm.

College was everything I expected. I went to college in the small town of Clarksville , TN which is minutes away from the military base, Fort Campbell. My first few weeks in college were EVERYTHING! Tons of parties, cute boys and freedom. After enjoying all that college life had to offer for the first few months, I decided I was going to hunker down and focus on making the grades that would help me get to the life I envisioned. I envisioned myself being a young professional, working in media broadcasting and living somewhere like New York. You know, like a real life Mary Jane from the tv show Being Mary Jane. Long story short, I met a fine piece of man freshmen year, got pregnant and had to take the second year of college to regroup. This was the first time in my newfound adult life that I felt like a failure. I felt like not only had I let my family down but I also let myself down. I declared to anyone who would listen that I was not going to be the chick to go off to college and get pregnant, but guess what? I was that chick.

It wasn't until three years later that I was able to step back out and re-enroll in college, this time enrolling into an accelerated adult program. I made up my mind when I enrolled that no matter what, I was completing the program and finishing what I had started. I was not going to let my family nor myself down. By that time I had two kids and one on the way. I kept that promise to myself and 2 1/2 years later I walked across the stage to receive my Bachelor's degree in Business & Organizational Development. That day all three of my children were in the audience cheering for me as I achieved my goal. One year later I enrolled in a masters' program and graduated in one year with a Master's of Fine Arts in Creative Writing.

During my years as an undergraduate student I searched for careers that matched my personality and my passion for helping others achieve their goals. I discovered life -coaching programs and was exposed to the coaching industry. At that time I could not fathom being a business owner and working independently as a coach. The only thing I could think about during that time was that I needed to get a job and make enough money to support my growing family. I could not see outside of the box of the "societal norm" of get an education, take that education and get a good job, work at that job for 30 plus years, retire and live happily ever after.

I graduated and did just that; I looked for a job. It took me several years before I landed a job that I actually liked. I landed a great opportunity to work for a startup Insurance brokerage firm that also had a tech part of the business. I took a role on the tech side dealing with client implementation, retention, analyzing and assisting with software improvements and overall client success. We worked hard, but we played even harder. I learned that insurance and tech professionals could be some of best people to work and party with. I was making enough money to support my family and even had flexibility as a mother to attend school events and take the time I needed to meet my responsibilities as a mother.

Even with all of the benefits of my job, I eventually started to feel as though I was unfulfilled in my career. I knew that I was not operating in my full potential and my full purpose. The long nights at work got longer and I went into a mild depression. I started to seek ways to bring that joy into my life. I created a blog hoping that would help to share my gifts with the world. That didn't work. I created a non-profit to work with young girls. That was fulfilling, but still was not enough. I tried for years to get the life coaching dream out of my mind, but the more I pushed it away the more it came back to me. Countless friends and family members told me I should be a counselor or a life coach because I was able to help them accomplish their goals or motivate them to be better.

January 2015 I got out of my own way. I decided that no matter what, I was going for it. I researched life- coaching programs and I was almost discouraged by the cost of some of the programs. I almost felt defeated again until I ran across a program that offered partial scholarships. How many of us know that when you set your mind on something and really go after it full force, the universe has a way of opening doors? The program was supposed to take nine months, but due to the death of a close family member that set me back emotionally, it took me eleven months. Once I completed the program I told myself that no matter what, I was stepping out on faith and giving this everything I had. I knew I had to take risks and throw ideas out there that may be unconventional, but they had the potential of being either great wins or great losses.

I sat my husband down and advised him that I am doing this because I feel a burning desire in my soul to do this. I explained to him that I could not sit on my gift any longer. I could no longer tell myself that I will do it when the kids are grown and gone. I couldn't wait; I had to do this and it had to be at that time! We talked about the support that I would need in order to be successful in this as a wife and as a mother. I got this idea from a podcast I listened to by one of my mentors in my head, Mattieologie. In one of her business podcast she suggested sitting your significant other down and telling them what would be needed from them tin order for you to be successful as a business owner. Moment of transparency: it didn't go down as smoothly as I pictured it when Mattie said it. I pictured I would sit him down and tell him something to the tune of, "Babe, I need your support as I venture down this path that I must take." I thought he would be open and reply with something supportive like, "no problem babe, whatever you need I'm here." That's not how that went at all. I started off telling him in my excited and passionate tone that I needed his support. I explained that this meant that some nights he would have to pick the kids up and prepare dinner while I focused on building my business and meeting with clients. He did not respond the way I had hoped and imagined. He asked me why would he have to do that and what exactly I hoped to accomplish and so many other questions that I did not have the answers to at the time. I did not know because I was in the beginning and exciting stages of starting a business. I was feeling the excitement from all of the self-help books, Instagram quotes and podcasts. I wasn't prepared for his response and it pissed me off. It didn't deter me; it lit a fire in me. At that moment I decided that I was not going to let anything or anyone, husband, kids, mama or anything or anyone else keep me from doing the work and making this transition.

Honey, I will tell you that when you're on a mission to your success the enemy (which could be yourself or a spiritual force) is on a mission too. That mission is to kill, steal and destroy your dreams. Once I made up my mind that I was going to do this in full faith no matter what, things started to happen. My kids who typically behave well in school and get decent grades started to get poor progress reports and I began getting calls from their teachers regarding problems with their behavior. There was tension between my husband and I and my job started to get shaky and a bit unstable. There have been many times that I've thought that it would be easier if I just settled into a "normal" life and work a "normal" job, but my drive and my passion will never let me settle for that. I've had to find creative ways to motivate my children, my husband and myself so that this can work.

When I stepped out and decided that I was going to do this I made a vow that no matter what hardships or what life happens, I am going to go after this with everything in me. I had no choice; my passion wouldn't let me rest. By declaring that out loud, I knew that the universe would hear it and not only would that help my goals to manifest but I also knew that it would also draw out detractors.

I told myself that it didn't matter who supported my vision. I was going to support it and guess what? The people whom I thought would support me did not. Instead of getting angry, I have kept it moving and eventually they will see that this is real and not just another crazy idea that I had.

When I tell you in the past year I have faced some of my toughest trials and have had to push through things that would have broken my spirit and my grit about seven to ten years ago.

I strongly believe that everything happens in God's perfect timing and HE knew that I was ready and can handle all that comes my way now. I've matured from that girl that was easily broken. Had I started this journey 10 years ago, I would not have made it too far because my faith was weak. Now I'm war ready and I know that to be successful it's going to take more than a pretty face and cute smile. This thing will take hard work, sleepless nights and one tired mama.

I can't tell you the excitement I felt when I signed my first client. I could not believe that someone trusted and believed in me enough to pay me for my services. Helping others achieve their goals had been something I did for free for so long. I had been giving others the truth about why they won't get to the finish line without a transformation and actually give them the tools to make that transformation happen. Now someone was paying me to do this; something I already loved. Doing what you love and are passionate about is the absolute best feeling in the world. It is right up there next to marrying your best friend or the birth of a child.

I get that feeling every time I sign a new client or at the end of every client session when I see their smiles and their goal journals full of to-do's. It is this feeling that helps me push past my limits. It is this feeling that makes the long nights worth it. It is the look I see in my husband and children's eyes when they see their mom/wife chase her dreams while still being very much a part of the day to day of their lives.

I went from not knowing if I would even get one client to having a full client list and having a full calendar of client sessions, networking events and continuously growing my brand. Me- the girl, from every hood in Nashville, is using my God given gifts to help others see their full potential and go after the things they want. For that, I will continue to push through and go hard.

In spite of the hardships I've experienced both personally and professionally in my short time as a business owner, I'm ready to take my brand to the next level. Ready to help my clients step out of stagnation and step into growth. Ready to live my dreams with my eyes wide open. I'm here for the good and the bad that I'm sure will come along with creating a successful business. I'm here for the failures and success that I will have to experience as I know it is inevitable with growth.

As a wife and mother my goal is to continue to grow my business, but also to continue to find a way to balance my family life and my business life. I want to be the example that my children look to of a woman who beat all of the odds, went after what she wanted and made it happen, no matter what. In being this example they will see how I make it all work even when there are times I have to reschedule client meetings because my 10 year old has a unscheduled basketball game or because my husband's schedule won't allow for him to pick the kids up from school. I am an example that it is possible through planning, being flexible and knowing that good comes in spite of the bad.

If you're a working mother, mompreneuer or aspiring momprenuer, my advice to you is to keep pushing. Life happens and you will always be dealing with life whether you're stepping into your purpose or working for someone who is living in their purpose. You will always have things that you can use as excuses as to why you're not doing the things you want to do or living your dreams. Don't let those things be the reason you never experience dreaming with your eyes wide open.

In the instance that you need help with that just remember that I am Kendra Garcia, owner of kendragarcia.com /Dream Life Coaching. I am a life and business strategist form Nashville, TN. How can I help you dream with your eyes wide open?

You can do anything if you JUST DO IT!

Your friend in your head and real life too,
Life Strategist KG

ABOUT THE AUTHOR

Kendra Garcia is a born and raised Nashvillain. After years of working in corporate America, she decided to take a leap out of the box to pursue her dream of becoming a world renowned Life & Business Coach, motivational speaker, Author & Mentor.

What makes Kendra a Life Strategist (Life coach)? Years of experience, persevering and overcoming her own trials and successfully beating the odds. Kendra Garcia has had to push through and overcome many obstacles including herself to accomplish her goals. She knows first hand about making excuses, putting off your dreams, living a less than desired life and being down right depressed with your current circumstances. She built her push through muscles by keeping her eyes focused on her goals and working hard to knock down every obstacle to make her dreams a reality.

It is her life experiences in addition with her formal training that has given Kendra the tools to help others overcome and achieve goals they never thought were possible, reach heights they never knew they were capable of and experience life transforming achievements.

When KG is not building her coaching brand, she enjoys being a wife to Francis Garcia, mom of 5 and watching HGTV with a good glass of wine.

Get to know her at KendraGarcia.com, follow her journey on social media: Instagram: @Lifestrategistkg, Twitter: @Lyfstrategistkg and Facebook: www.facebook.com/kendragarciaDLC

Chapter Two

Mompreneurs Levels of Success
By: Sabrina Wright

Let me start by being completely transparent, at one point in my life the stripper pole and my daughter was everything I stood for and it was my life. I didn't start off as such whereas I first started out taking corporate America by storm. Initially I was working at several different establishments such as Family Dollar, Payless Shoe store, and a debt consolidation company. I thought that I was on the chosen path of what any self-respecting individual should do. However the outcome was far from what I had expected. While working at the debt consolidation agency I grew weary of having to call delinquent clients daily and having to barter with them about paying their debts or to consider the option of consolidation. Most of the time I had to endure the clients' verbal abuse as they were often frustrated. Eventually I was fired because I became too lenient and just didn't take the job very seriously.

My position at Payless Shoe store was different from my previous job whereas I worked my way up to being a store manager. This was a great accomplishment for me at the time, but that feeling of accomplishment didn't last long. The feelings diminished as I was working longer hours for less pay. I somehow couldn't fathom the reason as to why I wasn't being paid what I was worth. I eventually submitted my resignation and found another job working at the Family Dollar. It didn't take long for me to attain a managerial status. This job was a bit more intensive, whereas I had a mirage of tasks to execute daily including: creating work schedules for the employees, ensuring that there wasn't any deviation from the payroll, and most importantly ensuring complete control of the inventory. It was twice the workload for yet again long hours and less pay. I remember being at work and coming across a few young ladies who seemed to have their wits about them. Being the curious person that I am, naturally I approached them and asked them about their occupation. To my surprise they told me about the exotic dancing industry.

I thought to myself that I wouldn't be a part of that as I already had a good thing going being a store manager and all. Fate would have it to where six months later, while I was getting ready to close the store and deposit the day's earnings to the bank, I was held up at gunpoint and robbed. Not very long after that ordeal I quit the job as I thought not only was I being held accountable for the incident, but I was working long hours for not much pay. I was once again frustrated and I no longer felt safe working there as corporate didn't deem it viable to employ security guards to protect their stores and their employees. For awhile I was uncertain of my next move. I then remembered speaking to the two young women and just figured that if they were exotic dancers, then I could do it as well and be my own boss at the same time.

So, everyday for four straight years I worked in several clubs within the Atlanta area. My goal was to earn at least five hundred dollars daily. I actually generated more as I mastered the art of how to make a man feel like he was the single most important person in the room.

I would normally head out to work at around 9pm. By that time my daughter and I would have spent a full day together and she wouldn't have noticed that I was gone. By the time I prepared to leave the house, she would have little spit bubbles running out of her mouth from being dead tired and asleep. I remember I would get to the club around 9:30pm and had to drink excessively and smoke marijuana before I would feel as if though I didn't have a care in the world. After I had my drinks and weed I would feel like I was the sexiest woman on the planet and I didn't care if a hundred men touched me every night, admired my beauty, wanted a seductive dance, or just wanted me to listen to their hopeless marital problems or problems with their kids. Whatever I had to do during that time, I did it to ensure that I made enough money to support my child and to live the life that I wanted. Sometimes that even meant me sleeping with a stranger for the money.

My state of mind at that time was that I simply didn't want to be a mom that worked all the time and couldn't see her child. On top of that I didn't want to be unable to really support her financially. I tried the lifestyle of working twelve to fourteen hour days at Family Dollar, a debt consolidation company, Payless Shoe Store, and other corporate America jobs while my daughter was at a daycare- away from me all day. I would like to add that I have no quarrels with corporate

America, it's just that it wasn't for me. I felt as though I could be my own boss and make a lot more money.

Childcare was becoming very expensive at one hundred and fifty dollars per week and I was only earning a salary of twenty-five hundred dollars per month before I started dancing. Considering my living expenses and the fact that I did not have any help, my salary was barely enough for us to survive. I was a full time single parent because the father of my child was and currently still is doing hard prison. I recognize that my situation is not an excuse for the lifestyle that I chose.

For four years strong I worked in several strip clubs in Atlanta. I also traveled to many places like Miami, South Carolina, Texas, Alabama, Alaska, Las Vegas, working as an exotic dancer. I earned over one hundred and fifty thousand dollars or more per year; however it still didn't give me the life I wanted for my daughter. I felt as though I found a way to earn more money to support her, but I was still away from her traveling with different men around the world and dancing. As a mother my mindset started to change. I didn't want my daughter to grow up and feel like she had to take her clothes off or sleep with strangers for money.

There came a time when I realized that I was leaving my daughter for my parents and day care providers to raise. Suddenly three years had passed and my daughter was walking and talking and doing so many interesting things that I was missing. It was at that point that I knew that I had to make a change in my life. After all, I left corporate America to become an entrepreneur who would have more money and time. I had more money but I didn't have the time. I felt I was losing myself to the men, drugs, sex, and alcohol. This was not how I imagined my life.

I began praying and asking God to help me find a better way to support my daughter and still spend time with her. I asked God for a husband who would love me for me, for my past, the present, and wherever the future would take me. I have always prayed and have been a lover of God because I grew up in the church. Unfortunately, I had gotten so far from God, and away from the church that club, drugs, sex, and money consumed me. One day, after leaving work on a Saturday night / Sunday morning I drove my car to this church parking lot and just poured my heart out to God until the church doors opened at 10:30am. I went into the church looking more like I was going to the club but I didn't care. I sat on the front pew because I was determined for God to give me some answers to my prayers. As fate would have it the sermon that was delivered was just for me. The pastor talked about how God loved me no matter what. He went on to say that our lives will be lived with imperfections but if I serve a perfect God that I can have the desires of my heart. I knew then that the message was for me, as I experienced a feeling like none other; it was as if though my spiritual eyes were awakened and I could feel the shift in my life happening.

I thank God he woke me up. After all that I have said, I never made any excuse(s) as to why I couldn't become the woman I am today. Everything I'm telling you was and still is my motivation. A year later following that prayer and a commitment to change along with four years into me being a single parent, I was married to an amazing man who currently serves in our United States military. I met him in the strip club where I was working. I remember the day I met him as though it were yesterday. He came in the club looking quite handsome and debonair in his military attire. He looked like he was lost so I walked over and asked him if he would be interested in getting a dance. He said yes without hesitation and I worked my body magic. He enjoyed the few dances so much that he asked me to go home with him and I did for a large fee. It turned into more than one night and three months into the amazing relationship I jokingly asked him to be my husband. It later turned into reality because we were married.

He has been very supportive in my decision to be an entrepreneur; however, I think he got more than he expected. Let me explain. I am not your typical woman as I have a fire down that has been buried deep within since I was a little girl. I have always known that I *Deserve to Win* so I moved out of my mother's house at the early age of seventeen on my journey to "figuring it out". I truly felt and still feel as though there is more to life than just going to work, coming home, and paying bills. I believe that life should be lived and experienced. In my opinion, why else would there be so many faucets of life such as different countries, states, even planets if it wasn't for myself or anyone else to experience. I believe that if my mind can think of it, then my physical being should be able to experience it.

So, I started on this journey of "figuring it out" since age seventeen. It was rough but, I didn't want to live by my parents' rules any longer. I felt as though I was grown. I wanted the freedom of being able to come and go as I pleased, do whatever I wanted to do whenever I wanted to do it. I no longer wanted to do chores because I felt as though that was beneath me. At that age, I felt as though my parents didn't see me for me and to them I was nothing more than just a child. They simply said it was either their way or the highway; the typical response of any loving parent. I made a conscious decision and chose the highway! In doing so, I can honestly say that I don't regret any of it because it made me who I am today and will mold the person that I am becoming.

As I mentioned earlier, I grew up in the church as a little girl. Whenever I attended Sunday school, my Sunday school teacher would often talk about abundance and freedom. I decided early that I wanted the abundance that my Sunday school teacher talked about in the Bible. I yearn for that freedom that the word of God talks about so I am spending my natural life trying to achieve that freedom. I went from being an exotic dancer earning six figures a year to losing everything, then getting married only to live an average typical life. You know that average life when you live paycheck- to - paycheck, budgeting every dime, not really buying what you want but what you can afford. Maybe taking one family vacation a year that it took you a year to save up for and even then, you still can't have the fun you want because of financial restrictions. Further my husband not being able to buy the things he wants because he now has a family to support.

I am not average so I decided to write down what I wanted out of life. I believe that I can have it because of the faith that I have in the God that I serve. I began to act daily with a plan to win and with persistence and dedication I haven't fallen short of any of my goals. I have the luxury of owning several failed businesses like a hair salon, moving company, and a boutique. I called it a luxury because it was in my failed businesses that I found my purpose and that is to help people get back up. I am a professional at getting back up. Now I don't have to fall because in all my resilience I have learned how to build a much firmer and stronger foundation. I have been dubbed as the *"**Lifestyle Architect**"*. I help people to plan, build, develop, and profit from their gifts. My slogan is I help people *"cash in on their passion"*. Whatever people's passion may be, I am the architect who helps people build a strong foundation which ensures that they don't fall. If people need to establish a Limited Liability Company (LLC), Trademark, copyright, or help with finding their passion, I am the "architect" for the job. If people have a need or desire to write a book I have a publishing company that they can utilize. I also teach people how to self-publish, I ghost write and I show people how to profit from their book. Anyone can write a book but it takes a certain type of person to be able to sell a book.

I have a thirty-one day affirmation book called *"You Deserve to Win"*. This book was just a journal of affirmations that I personally used to go from average to above average. I said these affirmations for ninety days consecutively and in ninety days my life was barely recognizable. I went from depending solely on my husband to earning over thirty thousand dollars in those ninety days in a health and wellness company that I collaborated with. Also within that ninety- day time frame I started an organization to help other entrepreneurs start their businesses and I published a book. I was so amazed at what using the affirmations did for my life that I felt compelled to share them in a book in order to help others achieve the same. I truly believe that our journeys and life experiences are not for us to hoard but to help others. I am a lifetime student and everything that I learn I try to implement quickly. If it works then I teach it, so that I can be of value to someone else. Zig Ziegler is quoted, *"You can get everything out of life you want if you will just help enough other people get what they want."* I live by this; therefore I live life serving others.

Due to the many obstacles that I was faced with while in corporate America, I decided to become a *"Mompreneur"* who is of service to others. I have chosen to serve others because there was once a time when I was the one looking for information. My experience included others giving me the run around or giving me information that wasn't of any value. I had people give me information that made me do a detour around my goals because they were afraid that I may excel higher than they would. I even had a "good friend" refuse to tell me how to do something because she said no one told her how to do. She felt that withholding this information would make it harder for me and allow me to appreciate my lesson. I was stunned as I couldn't believe that my friend and others were so selfish with information and resources.

I was alone trying to make decisions on what I should invest. Many of my investments failed because I didn't have a coach or mentor. I would also be the person with no money, a plethora of ideas, and just needed someone to believe in my vision(s). After years of trials and tribulations, I decided to be the change I wanted to see. I am the woman who will invest in someone's vision. I am the woman that learns new skills and then imparts that knowledge with every hope and intention of helping someone else gain more knowledge and income. I am the woman who will walk with you or lead the way because I know what it feels like to walk alone. I am here to help anyone and everyone. You can contact me www.sabrinawright.net in order to become a part of a network of men and women who love God and turn their passions into a paycheck.

Being an entrepreneur is the best decision I have made because now as a *"Mompreneur"* I can see the little details of my daughter's life that most parents miss because they must work so much. I get to go on school field trips, attend Parent Teacher's Association (P.T.A) meetings, eat lunch with my daughter at school just because, and volunteer to help her teacher. I get to live a life from which I don't need a vacation. When I work from my phone or computer my daughter is right there with me. My daughter gets to attend home parties, watch me record my information and inspiration videos. She even participates in some of the videos. My daughter gets to help me prepare for my workshops and she even knows how to plan, decorate, and facilitate the workshops.

The most beautiful thing about being an entrepreneur is that it leads me to believe that I am raising my replacement. Knowing that causes me to constantly set the bar higher in being that example for my daughter. One of the ways in which I have set the bar higher was by illustrating to my daughter that even as an entrepreneur and a busy mom and wife, I was also capable of going back to school and completing my degree in Medical Science. It wasn't easy and there were times when I had to enlist the help of my husband who would sometimes be dog faced tired after a long day's work, but through perseverance, dedication, and commitment I was successful.

My daughter doesn't have to watch the television to be inspired by celebrities such as Beyoncé, Niki Minaj, or Lil Kim. She can look at me and be inspired. My daughter often looks at me and says,"I want to be *this* version of you mommy when I grow up, not the exotic dancer version." My daughter tells me how proud she is of my strength and tenacity to never give up. She tells me that I am her role model. She doesn't have to go out and look for a job when she has watched her mother create her own path and her own income, and that right there is the most beautiful part of being an entrepreneur. Being an example to my daughter that she "*can, be, do*", or have whatever she wants makes the daily fight to thrive as an entrepreneur all worth it.

Don't get me wrong, being an entrepreneur isn't always pretty. You will need a great support system because as an entrepreneur you don't always make money right away. That's why I thank God for my husband and family. When I decided to stop working in the strip club bills still had to be paid. My husband sacrificed his entire paycheck sometimes to make certain that he invested in my dreams and goals. He has invested in so many things that honestly didn't work the way we planned. But we didn't stop there. He continues to invest in my personal development and business ventures because he understands that my bank account only grows when I grow.

However, we are continually investing in books, mentorship, and different workshops to ensure that I grow with our money. As an entrepreneur, you have to work on you and the value you offer to the world, because to be completely honest your income will be in direct proportion to the service and value you have to offer others. For example, if you have a corporate America job they are paying you based on how valuable they feel you are to their company -which is dependent on your education and skills. The more valuable you are to the company the more money they will pay you. If the company feels as though you are no longer a valued asset or service to their company they fire you. That is just how it works. It works just like that for an entrepreneur with the exception you will never get paid for doing nothing. That is why it is imperative that you are continuously learning and growing so you never run out of value to add to the world. In return you will never have to worry about not having money another day in your life.

    Being an entrepreneur will be all worth it once you figure out your niche. My slogan is *"find your niche and get rich"*. Once you find that niche and your heart is pure, you will see God do some amazing and wonderful things in your life. You won't recognize your life because you will have so many blessings coming your way. You will begin to attract the right people and resources in your life. This book is evidence of attracting the right people into your life. I get a chance to share my story with other amazing authors who may have the luxury of failed jobs, marriages, businesses, etc but decided to never give up. My personal advice to anyone is this: no matter how many businesses you try that don't work out in your favor, don't give up. Find someone that you can collaborate with on different thoughts, methodologies, various courses of actions and just take that leap of faith.

I have learned through faith and the reading of the word of God that if one can take one thousand a flight but two can take ten thousand a flight (Deuteronomy 32:30). God wants us to collaborate with one another. It's more than just building our businesses, as we must think of it as building the Kingdom of God. After all the Bible also teaches us to do everything as if we are doing it for God; to build the body of Christ whereby the body of Christ comprises of you and me. Therefore, if you really take the time to seek your purpose and do everything you can to ensure you are the best at what you do, there will be no man or woman on this earth that can stop you because you ***"Deserve to Win!"***.

ABOUT THE AUTHOR

Sabrina is a mother, wife, and an entrepreneur. She plays an active role in her community both independently and through her church to help the less fortunate and provide leadership and guidance to the youth.

Sabrina earned her Bachelor of Science in Biology, obtained her license as a Master Cosmetologist, and also received an Associate in Applied Science. She has always enjoyed starting and running businesses and has been doing so since she was seventeen years old.

Sabrina owns and operates several businesses. She is the Chief Executive Officer of Bree's Beauty Box LLC, Wright Connections Global, Boss Diva Moving and Sabrina Wright Publishing Co. In addition, she continues to grow her global empire through her director level within a health and wellness company called Total Life Changes. When Sabrina is not focused on the constraints of the office, she loves to read the Bible and get spiritually in tune, work out at the gym and spending time with her daughter.

The things she loves most in life are a healthy relationship with God, her family, and her daughter. She thinks of herself as a go-getter, filled with optimism of the impossible, and very outgoing. She surrounds herself with like-minded and spiritual individuals. She pushes people to pursue success by encouraging them that they deserve to win.

Sabrina is the author of the book "You Deserve to Win" and "The Power to Publish". She and her family reside in Atlanta, Georgia.

Chapter Three

PowHer of Perseverance
By: Tye Miles

I finally landed an opportunity to fulfill my dream of being a Runway Fashion Model, my bags were packed and last on the list was a clean bill of health from my physician. As I sat in the clinic waiting for my name to be called, I remember thinking, "It's happening, my dream is really coming true!" The nurse called my name and then she began the typical routine of taking my blood pressure, weighing me, etc. However, before I could be seated back in the waiting area the nurse called my name again and asked me one single question that changed my life forever, "Did you know that you were pregnant?" Jaw dropped, heart stopped, legs numb. I was 16 years old and pregnant. This reality hit me hard like a sack of pennies.

I was a high school student, I had a bright future in front of me, I had been given the opportunity to model and I was pregnant. My family and friends were shocked. Nobody expected to hear this news of an academic standout primed to be tapped into The National Honor Society. Life got harder with the onset of my pregnancy. It was difficult enough dealing with my personal feelings of disappointment and failures, that emotional distress was topped with being denied induction into the National Honor Society. Despite having to get a job to prepare for a baby and studying extra hard to keep my GPA up, I still wasn't considered a "proper role model" worthy of being inducted. The gestures, remarks, and taunting of my peers combined with the sadness and pain etched on my parents' faces made this overwhelming reality even more challenging.

Deflated, depressed and discouraged was my constant state of emotions. I constantly felt hopeless. For several months I privately battled suicidal thoughts and my self-esteem was dropping like a brick in water. I was desperately in search of something to anesthetize the pain. It is nothing short of the grace of God that I am still alive and in my "right mind". One day after leaving church I decided that enough was enough. I didn't like the downward spiral that my life was seemingly taking. It felt like a black hole was sucking the life from me. It became imperative that I somehow needed to find hope and once again believe in the bright future that was still in front of me. I made a decision to face the young woman and all the negative emotions in the mirror. I decided I no longer wanted to subscribe to a "victim" mentality. I define "victim" mentality as: when you feel that your circumstances or situation is a justified excuse to give in or give up on your dreams, goals and ambitions. You blame yourself and others for why you aren't successful. You seek the attention of others to entertain your pity party. You wallow in regret. You sit around complaining while taking little to no responsibility for your own life and your contributing decisions. I changed the direction of my mindset and decided I was not a failure because of past decisions and circumstances. Going forward, I chose to be a "victor" and not play the role of "victim" in my life story.

As one of my favorite scriptures reads:

1 Corinthians 15:57 (New International Version) But thanks be to God! He gives us the victory through our Lord Jesus Christ.

Once I decided that I would no longer live in the shadows of condemnation, shame, statistics, other people's expectations or even my own failures, my life officially changed. I realized that what mattered most at this place in my journey was my beautiful baby girl. Out of the darkness I rose because as I stared into my daughter's eyes I could see that she needed me, I was important to her, she became my 'WHY!' I persevered, survived, overcame and believed in myself because of her. My past failures, disappointments and fears were small compared to my future with her. I knew I had to be focused on becoming a person she could be proud of and depend on.

My current reality helped me to put away my immature thinking and habits. I was faced with a tougher task. I remembered asking myself while looking down at my daughter as she rested in her crib, "How am I going to build a future for us?" This question shaped my life then as much as it continues to shape my life now. I began to seek wise counsel and direction regarding the next steps of securing gainful employment to provide for my family. I wanted more than what my previous jobs offered. I worked several jobs during this season of my life and was fired from some too. Being an employee wasn't quite going over well with me, I wasn't fond of the limits and restrictions of working for a company. I didn't enjoy someone else determining my earning potential; I wanted to be in control of that. I was constantly feeling that my values were being compromised; working more hours for more money but neglecting time with my family. I desired the freedom to be an active mother, and that was more than requesting time off for school trips and using 'nonexistent' sick days. If I was going into work while sick I would rather be working for myself instead of a company with no regard for my health or that of my daughter. I pondered heavily which path would get me to my desired lifestyle.

I received valuable advice on whether or not I should go off to college or pick up a trade. Nevertheless, the most impactful answer I was seeking came from within me. I was lead to go on a 21 day spiritual fast, during this fast I asked God several specific questions. As I spent time daily in prayer, reading my Bible, and journaling, God answered every single question.

Some of the questions I sought clarity regarding was:

1. *What is my purpose?*
2. *Who did you create me to be?*
3. *What natural gifts, talents & abilities did you give me?*
4. *What is the next "right move" I should make?*

I specifically remember one of my journal entries: *My purpose is connected to my passion. My passion is represented by my pain. Whatever areas of my life that has caused me the greatest amount of pain will also be the areas where I will have the greatest power and influence. And when my purpose is driven by my passion then prosperity will result. PURPOSE ~ PASSION ~ PROSPERITY*

At the end of these 21 days of fasting I had a deeper understanding of the direction of my life. More importantly I had clarity and confidence regarding my natural gifts, talents and abilities. I enrolled in cosmetology school that very same week, but daily I continued to seek direction for my life. I wrote my plans down with dates by each one. I was intentional in my actions to ensure each goal was met.

When I arrived at Lawson State Community College to enroll in classes I was greeted with a familiar face, Ms. Gwendolyn Hunter. It was like déjà vu! I remember sitting in the back of her class as a little girl when my mother attended night classes for cosmetology. I remember thanking God for leaving me breadcrumbs. Yes, like breadcrumbs from my favorite fairytale Hansel and Gretel; this was a gentle reminder that I was on the right path. Cosmetology school proved itself to be both challenging and rewarding; there were times I was pushed to my limits. My instructor was very tough on me, combine that with the kinks of being a working single parent. In spite of its difficulty, completing college was an extremely proud moment in my life, crossing that stage brought me one step closer to my plans of securing a brighter future. Curiosity and discovery seems to sum this chapter of my life.

My go-to scripture during this period was:

Matthew: 7:7 (New King James Version) "Ask, and it will be given to you; seek, and you will find; knock, and it will be opened to you.

It was time to take the next step. To make it all official I had to pass my state board examination; suddenly fear stepped in. I was so frightened that I would fail my exam because my mother had shared many stories of how hard it was to pass. She told me that she hadn't passed it herself. For that reason, I didn't take my examination until five years later. Let's talk about these five years.

There's something about feeling stuck between a rock and a hard place. I was now a newlywed and expecting the birth of my second daughter in just two short months. My husband and I decided that I should submit my notice for maternity leave because of complications from Gestational Diabetes. Being at home would allow me to better monitor the illness and prepare for our new addition. I was happy to not have to hit the time clock. I was even more thrilled about spending as much time as possible with my oldest daughter before I gave birth. My excitement of being a "stay at home" mom soon ended with the news of my husband being laid off from his job. We lost our income and medical insurance. I found myself applying for

Medicaid, welfare, choosing a new doctor and hospital all with less than one month before the birth of my second child. We went from working hard to build a firm foundation for our family to barely holding on by threads. We had to reach out to family and friends to help keep food on the table and roof over our heads. However, the support of family and friends didn't last long. We reluctantly decided it was necessary to file for bankruptcy. This was one of the most frustrating choices I remember making. I had spent the last two years of my life crossing off paid debts on my credit report to better my credit score.

    I remember asking myself. "How could this be happening?" I was only earning less than 15K a year. I had sacrificed eating out, buying new shoes and clothes and even denying my daughter new toys and activities. I was angry and full of regret. I couldn't stop thinking about the thousands of dollars I spent paying my credit card and medical bills and every sacrifice we had made. The very thing I was trying to avoid had happened; we lost our home, our cars and suffered major damage to our credit. Disheartened, I was reminded of my childhood. I grew up living in a public housing community, raised with my three sisters by my mom. My mom was my superhero. She worked two, three and sometimes four jobs to keep us fed and clothed. We always had a roof over our heads although sometimes there would be no power or water. I remember creating a candle kit because coming home to a pink "disconnect" slip on the door had become the norm. In spite of the many struggles of my childhood, my mom always knew how to make us smile. She would prepare special meals and create silly games that filled the rooms with laughter and our hearts with joy. I could see the sign of being a hardworking single-mother on her face. I also saw an abundance of love, strength and resilience. I am my mother's daughter! I knew that if she could keep her head up and keep going during years of hard circumstances then so could I. Encouraged to create a different life for myself and my children I knew I had to keep chasing my dreams of being a successful hairstylist and salon owner. Though, it seemed like a very distant reality from the scenery of my situation, I started to speak of my vision in the midst of everything going on. Just talking about it inspired me to keep my mind elevated above my trials.

Those that were close to me knew that I would persevere and shine like gold regardless of the adversity. Soon I realized that my words had built this amazing invisible world that felt so real that I knew it was only a matter of time before it would in fact be my reality. Though I could not see my business with my human eyes yet, it was real in my spirit and I believed in the power of my vision. My words literally were the breath, blood and spirit of my entrepreneurial success. On the days my vision felt far away from me I reflected back on my journey to remind myself of how far I had come and of the great plans I had written about my future. Someone seemed to always call or stop me to tell me how they were eagerly waiting on me to be their stylist. They encouraged me to keep pushing. My husband believed in me so much that he began buying items for my business and storing them in our garage. He would not let me settle for going back to hitting the time clock. He had started a new career in management and insisted that I pursue my vision. He reminded me that according to:

James 2:17 (New King James Version) "Thus also faith by itself, if it does not have works, is dead."

I could believe in the promises of God and write down the vision and plans that were in my heart all I wanted to but until I took all the steps of the process, my vision would never manifest. I took comfort in the belief that everything I was experiencing was necessary for me to become the person I needed to be for the journey ahead. It was in this moment that I realized how real my fear was; at this crossroad I took the road of faith over fear. For five years I found myself paralyzed by my mother's fear. Upon taking the state board examination I passed the first time! I couldn't believe how long I allowed myself to suffer at the hands of fear. And here I learned in life that sometimes you just have to, 'DO IT AFRAID'!

"Being average isn't good enough. I let others get by, but not you. I believe you have more on the inside of you. I'm harder on you because I see excellence in you!" said Ms. Hunter, one of my college professors. Ms. Hunter showed me the importance of an excellent work ethic, strong habit of integrity and having high expectations. I hold myself, my family and my business partners to a great level of accountability and excellence because of the example she was to me.

It was this mentality that I started my career as a Hairstylist. I rented a booth at a well-known salon. I didn't really know what to expect as an entrepreneur but I learned many hard lessons fast. Building a clientele was extremely difficult and I found myself rarely being able to pay the $75 weekly booth rent. I was working for other stylists in the salon shampooing their clients' hair. I had to take the undesirable clients that nobody would even consider styling just to make ends meet. Unfortunately, the salon had a competitive, low moral atmosphere that wasn't very professional or well managed. I was in a perpetual state of frustration; this was not my idea of the successful business model that I had imagined. After nearly seven months of the entrepreneurial life, I was strongly considering an "8 to 5" job although ultimately I knew that was what I did not want.

Something was not right and I had to figure out what was wrong and fast; back to the drawing board. My first line of defense was to scale back my salon schedule, longer hours was not profitable for me. I took some time to really focus on what I desired my business brand to be, the clientele I wanted to serve and how I wanted to serve them. Yes, this was a sacrifice financially because I loss income; however it was a defining decision in my career. I began to target my ideal clientele, and I exceeded their expectations in the areas of service and style. As my clientele grew steadily I was able to not only become more financially stable, but I found myself standing tall above the challenges that were once weighing me down. This is FREEDOM people! Financial freedom, time freedom, stress freedom and the relief I felt was indescribable. I started saving money aggressively. I began creating memories with my family because I could now spend time away from the salon without fear of my family lacking. I could feel the emotional bruises of my past evaporating. I felt confident that I would be able to provide a very different lifestyle for myself and my family. My newly discovered business model was working really well, even in the midst of the worst financial crisis since the Great Depression of the 1930s. In less than 10 months after going back to the drawing board, I went from barely being able to pay $75 weekly booth rent to earning a six figure income! I am NOT an overnight success. My past obstacles and adversities taught me how to persevere, be disciplined and stay focused. I applied those key principles to my entrepreneurial journey and with consistency; this resulted in my success. Achieving this milestone in my career was incredibly hard, unbelievable and amazing. With continued success in the forecast I made the decision to open my own salon.

  Realizing that my dream of ownership was just around the corner, I had to deal with the burden of having filed bankruptcy and the effect it will have on my decision to open a salon. I was fully convinced that everything was going to work for my benefit. I encountered several obstacles as I set out to open my salon. I was denied approval for several buildings. I was told I didn't have enough liquid assets and my credit score was too low. After searching for what seemed like an eternity, I found a building in a location that I loved with a "For Rent" sign on the door. I met with the business owner, and as we walked through the building I was explaining to her the salon design and layout.

She was excited and she believed in my vision. She was so confident that I was the perfect fit that she called the owner of the building, only to hear, "I'm sorry, 'Black-owned' beauty salons are open one day and closed the next." The tears welled up in my eye as I left those doors with yet another rejection. But before my car reached the end of the street I received a call saying that the building was mine! The building owner would not lease the building to me but allowed the business owner (the lady) to sublease the remaining two years of her contract to me. She wanted me have the building because she believed in my vision and felt my passion. Now that I had a building, most of the bids for the contracts to build out the salon were far out of my budget. I decided to take on as many DIY projects as I could manage, saving my budget for jobs that had to be done by licensed and bonded professionals. I reached out to family and friends for support, once again I saw how little my support system believed in my vision. I firmly believe that God will give you what you need, when you need it. Only a select few of my family members tirelessly worked alongside me to help manifest my salon. Just nine months after being discharged from bankruptcy, The Signature Salon (MY OWN SALON) opened its doors for business in December 2009. My past wasn't pretty and there were many flawed and blemished days. I experienced being a single parent while in high school, disappointments, failures, low self-esteem and financial hardships. I'm thankful for each experience because they taught me valuable lessons that shaped my entrepreneurial mindset.

As I reflect back on my journey I discovered eight keys that have helped me build and balance a successful lifestyle as an entrepreneur. I call them the "Super 8 to Surviving Entrepreneurship".

1. Know Your Own Worth! ~ There is tremendous power in knowing who you are and what you have to offer. It doesn't matter how many businesses offer the same service as you. They can't do it like you because you are the only one of YOU there is in the entire universe. Now that's MAGICAL! Sometimes we crave the approval of others, while it may feel good to be accepted, don't get used to it. On this journey of life you will be misunderstood and talked about. But remember people only talk about the things that interest them. Know undoubtedly your own value. Learn how to encourage yourself. Celebrate your individuality. Remember that your level of expectation determines your level of disappointment. Monitor your level of need of acceptance from others. This protects you from the disappointment associated with rejection. Be willing to put in the work to earn trust. Understand you and your services will not be for everyone. Always guard your heart and don't allow rejection to take residence. Be mentally prepared to swim through an ocean of 'NO's' to catch your 'YES' fish – Tye Miles

2. Either You Win or Get Wiser! ~ Past disappointments and failures should not define you, allow them to refine you. Learn from the past and be strengthened by it. Remember that you can never speak from a place that you have no experience. Gain expertise from your past experiences.

3. Define, Delete, And Declare! ~ Define who you want to be. Write in detail what you want from your lifestyle. Create a vision board and journal. Delete negative thoughts (internal and external). Refer back to your vision and allow it to help you to determine your habits and make vital decisions along your journey. Surround yourself with people, places and things that support your vision. Intentionally make positive declarations about you and your vision.

4. Don't Give Up! ~ The ability to persevere is imperative to success. Entrepreneurs must be able to endure adversity. The only difference between the person that accepts failure and the person that succeeds is simple; THEY NEVER QUIT. Your only job in the face of adversity is to get to the other side of it. Just keep going!

5. *Do It Afraid!* ~ Not knowing is scary. But not starting because of what you don't know is even scarier. By definition an entrepreneur is a risk-taker. Remember there is no reward without risk.

Being a mompreneur is scary. Having other human beings depending on your success to provide food, shelter, guidance and affirmation is a huge responsibility. As entrepreneurs we eat what we kill. This leaves no room for fear because we have to be leaders and providers. Be confident! Have faith! Give it your all and you won't have any regrets. "You don't have to be great to get started, but you have to get started to be great." – Zig Ziglar

6. *Your Network Is Your Net Worth!* ~ Build healthy relationships. I don't believe we were created to journey solo. For a mother and entrepreneur (Mompreneur), relationships are valuable. Teamwork definitely makes the dream work. There was once a time when I did everything myself. Honestly, I took pride in being able to do so without depending on others. If you are in this place you are robbing yourself of success. Your dream should be so big and create such a demand that you have to seek out the help of others, train, elevate and delegate others. As my business grew I had to humble myself and ask for HELP! My family is a huge part of my support system. They help with my kids' activities, appointments and even cooking meals. My colleagues and salon staff are awesome! They come early and stay late. They help to ensure an exceptional product/ service is

delivered. They guarantee the salon experience is consistent whether I'm in the salon or away on business or vacation. My church family and friends lift me up in prayer and hold me down in the face of any circumstance. We 'Do Life' together! As I build my brand and business beyond the salon, my business network of mentors and professionals help push me even further into my destiny. The areas where I am weak they add value to me through wisdom, knowledge and guidance. They develop me so that I will be ready when even greater opportunities are presented. Building this network has allowed me to earn a greater income as well as create income for others; iron sharpens iron. When YOU win, Your TEAM WINS!

7. Preparedness Breeds Success! ~ I'm no different from anyone else when it comes to facing adversity, I've had my fair shares; especially as it relates to financial adversity. It has taught me to plan for the best and prepare for the worst. Financially speaking, my past experiences have left a bitter sting, I refuse to return to financial ruins, therefore, I save, save, save. I have a savings account as well as the following types of accounts: ***Retirement***: I pay into this account because one day I hope to sit back and enjoy the fruit of my labor. ***Emergency***: Three to six months of expenses saved back in the case of unforeseen financial hardships ***Investment***: I place money aside for future opportunities that may interest me. I want to make sure that I will be in position to invest without stress. Many people want success but do not have the wherewithal (finances, resources and assets) to make it happen. ***Play***: I reward myself, children, family and friends from this account. This account comes in handy when I want to reward good behavior, buy a toy or surprise them with a spontaneous trip to create a memory. ***Benevolence***: This account ensures that I'm positioned to be generous and lend a helping hand without expecting it back.

While I enjoy the pleasures that my current financial position allow, I intentionally consume less than I produce. I never spend all that I earn! Professionally speaking, know your stuff! Truly perfect your craft. Perform regular assessments of your strengths and weaknesses. Nurture and grow your strengths. Prune and cultivate your weaknesses. Learn everything there is to know about your trade. Read and listen to media that sharpens you. Surround yourself with people that make you feel like you don't know anything. Yes, that's right. If you are the smartest person in your circle then it's time to level up to the next circle. Get uncomfortable! Stay Ready! Don't get caught unprepared when opportunity comes knocking.

8. Consistency + Discipline = Results! This is my personal mantra. First I identified my brand. Next I recognized my niche clientele. Lastly, I intentionally worked to perfect my craft and experience. Be consistent in the quality of your product/ service. Be disciplined in your character. Be professional at all times. Never blur the lines with your clients. Remember to never chase money, always chase excellence.

Prosperity follows excellence!

My entrepreneurial journey has taught me so much. Each time I have the opportunity to share my story I am genuinely humbled when someone tells me how much they are inspired by my testimony. I am very intentional with being transparent about my entrepreneurial journey. I'm not special. The only difference between my success and your success is a made up mind and a commitment to never settle for less than what you feel deep within you are able to achieve. I've seen many stylists struggle to succeed. The Beauty Industry is a 56 billion dollar industry and growing. Being a Hairstylist can be a very lucrative business. However, I've witnessed many stylists treat it as no more than a side hustle, they are unbalanced. I find that many stylists are extremely creative and talented but lacking the necessary business wisdom and financial discipline. My desire to see other stylists achieve financial and time freedom has pushed me further into my destiny. It has expanded my business beyond the chair. I feel I've connected with a life purpose. In this season of success I truly believe that as I meet the needs of others I will simultaneously meet my own. I no longer merely live for FINANCIAL PROVISION but rather to FULFILL PURPOSE!

I end this chapter with the words from: *Isaiah 41:10 ISV "Don't be afraid, because I'm with you; don't be anxious because I am your God. I keep on strengthening you; I'm truly helping you. I'm surely upholding you with my victorious right hand."*

ABOUT THE AUTHOR

Committed to empowering female entrepreneurs, Tye Miles is a Business Consultant to hairstylists and beauty professionals that are ready to experience deeper levels of success in this industry. She is passionate about empowering women and helping them to develop more profitable brands while improving financial education.

Tye, Master Stylist of 15 years, excels in demonstrating the art of hair and healthy hair care. She has been a successful entrepreneur since 2008, owning and operating The Signature Salon of Birmingham, Alabama. Tye is a graduate of Lawson State Community College where she received her certification in Cosmetology. She successfully serves a clientele roster of Birmingham's elite, executives and professional women. Among her many achievements, Tye Miles was honored as an Outstanding Women of Color in Leadership by The Young Progressive Black Caucus of Alabama in 2016.

Furthering her personal brand beyond the salon, Tye

feels a sense of purpose and obligation to influence the next generation of women business leaders in the beauty industry. Realizing her purpose served as a catalyst to inspire and educate the next generation of beauty professionals. She helps them to cultivate their skills along with the discipline and strategy needed to create a lifestyle of flexibility and financial freedom.

Tye is currently creating educational products designed to equip, encourage and empower hairstylists and beauty professionals to achieve maximum results in their business.

Tye is available for speaking engagements and is always excited to share her purpose, passion and knowledge of this industry. She shares stories of personal challenges and business insight in a relatable tone that allows her to connect with her audience and motivate them to "live their potential

www.TyeMiles.com
Instagram:@thetyemiles
Facebook:www.facebook.com/thetyemiles/
LinkedIn: https://www.linkedin.com/in/tye-miles-08aa8946

Chapter Four

Just a Girl Who Decided to Chase Hers
By: Lakesha Reed-Curtis, MSN, RN

We all have dreams of having the best and being the best. But with the many obstacles we have as women, it can sometimes seem impossible to reach our destiny. But, if no one has ever told you that you can have it all let me be the first! I'd like to congratulate you if you have entered or will soon be entering the realm of being a mompreneur. I wish I could say the road to becoming a mompreneur was easy, but I like to keep it real! However, if I left out the fact that it was completely worth it, then I'd be selling you short.

Let me give you a little background information about myself before I dive into my experiences as a mompreneur. I am Lakesha Reed-Curtis, MSN, RN, and the owner of Allied Health Academy, Medical Solutions Academy, Inc., which was founded in 2011. I also recently started Dream ChasHers, a company that provides business coaching for new entrepreneurs. I have an amazing nine-year old son, KeShaun, and a beautiful baby girl, Madison, and have been married to my adoring husband Terrel for two years. I have been a Nurse for fourteen years and received both my Bachelor and Master degrees in Nursing at Winston-Salem State University. I am proud to report that I received my Masters in Nursing Education while being a mompreneur as well.

I always knew I would someday own my own business. I would go to work daily and tell my co-workers and friends my dreams and aspirations of being a business owner. They would laugh, but not in a bad way. They knew I would not be an employee for long! Even at that time I knew that you have to speak things into existence even if you are not so clear on the direction. However while speaking it into existence you must also take the first step to execute. My first step was leaving my hometown of Danville, Va. and moving to Charlotte, NC with my 1 ½ year old son in tow. We didn't have any family there and I had no clue who would care for my child while I was at work. I didn't let that stop me. I prayed, secured a pretty decent job as an Assistant Director of Nursing and we were out. Just like that. Fearless superwoman!

Unfortunately I didn't think the plan out so well. It was a little difficult to find a daycare provider that I was comfortable with so my mom kept my son in Virginia for about a month. It was one of the hardest things I ever had to do. However, I knew that I had to sacrifice a little to gain a lot. I eventually connected with the perfect daycare provider that cared for my son as if he were her own. Given the fact that I did not know anyone nor have a support system in Charlotte people ask me all the time why I chose to move to Charlotte. My answer is simple- I liked the city and it was still close to my hometown. Little did I know although I was not really far from home, this move would open my eyes to so much more. One of my first observations upon relocated was that it seemed as if no one worked!! I learned that the city was full of entrepreneurs.

Upon my relocation I knew more than ever that this was the lifestyle that I wanted. I needed the freedom to live on the edge a little, take business risks, and make my own choices without the constraints of a set schedule or someone else's rules. I don't think people realize how working for someone else consumes your whole life. All areas of my life were dictated by a work schedule. I became sick of asking for paid time off to take vacations, have a "me" day, or even run errands! And let's be honest, thirty minutes is just not enough time to enjoy a nice lunch. I had been bitten by the entrepreneur bug and I knew I couldn't work a regular 9-5 job long-term; I needed to make a change quickly!

I just had to figure out what type of business I wanted to own. I knew I wanted to help my community in a different way than what was already being done. Most importantly, I wanted to be home with KeShaun as much as possible. By the time I picked him up from daycare it would be dark outside and the day would be over. I felt as if I was missing so much of his life while I was working. It was during those times that I set a goal to be at home with him daily before he started Kindergarten. I wanted this freedom so badly. I would sit around and just pray for a business idea to come to me.

One night as I was lying in bed with KeShaun I had the idea to sell nursing scrubs. In that moment I hugged him so tight and began to jump up and down in the bed! He was three years old; I remember it all so well. I thought big, but started small. I began doing trade shows at local nursing homes and sold scrubs to most of my co-workers and nursing friends. Little did I know this was the start of my entrepreneurial journey! My good girlfriend would travel with me in my Toyota Camry, crammed in the car surrounded by the scrubs I was transporting up the road to sell. We still laugh about it to this day!

Selling scrubs was something I did on the side while I worked my full-time job. However, I needed and wanted so much more. I recognized that nurse aide programs were becoming a trend in North Carolina. This piqued my interest as I always had a passion for education and the desire to teach. Although I still had a full-time job, I quickly began researching the requirements and qualifications necessary to start a nurse aide program in Virginia. I didn't know when or how I would start this new venture, but I knew that I would.

As luck would have it, I was terminated from my job as Assistant Director of Nursing in November 2010. I was shocked, but I had a plan. Five short months later, in April 2011 Medical Solutions Academy opened its doors. God is amazing! I always liked education and I knew that I would one day go into nursing education; however I never imagined I would own my very own school. Years later and I still wonder if I hadn't been fired if I would have had the courage to eventually quit and follow my dream. It's hard for me to say, but at the time my back was against the wall. I refused to let another individual or company determine the fate of me and my family. In my eyes I didn't have any other option but to step out on faith and start MSA.

Let me be clear, I didn't have a huge bank account. Ok, let me be very clear- I didn't have a bank account. I started my business solely based on passion and not a lot of money. My money was in my brain; I knew it was coming. So here I was a single mom and an entrepreneur ready to take on this huge task! I worked day in and day out to make sure it was a success. I also put a little buzz in the community to let them know what I was starting. That was vital as it made it easier to obtain students upon the start of my program. Once my name was in the community, organizations sought me. They were watching me and what I was doing and I did not even know it. I've learned in business to always work hard for that particular reason- you never know who is watching.

Although being an entrepreneur has granted me the desired freedom to work as I please, we all know being the boss is not easy! Couple that with being a mom and you have reached a completely new level of lack of time. Every mompreneur will have her own set of rules and guidelines she lives by to balance her everyday life. My one and only rule is to place God first, family second, and THEN business. I live by this and try my best to follow this day in and day out. Anytime I tend to stray from this, it seems like my world spirals out of control. When things tend to go wrong I check myself to make sure I'm following my golden rule. If I find that I've switched that order, I'll immediately start praying and ask God to align my vision with His again. My purpose in starting my business was given to me through the talents with which God blessed me and He will forever come first in my life. My family is and will always be my main priority on Earth; therefore, although my business is my baby, it will always come third in my life.

Outside of my golden rule communication is a major key for both my personal life and business. If I have an urgent task at hand I make sure to communicate that to my family and/or office manager so they will be prepared to make accommodations. I strongly believe when I take the time to talk to my family about what I have going on in business, it makes them feel included and valued. In business I believe in boosting morale and having a strong rapport within my company. Communicating with my staff when I have personal matters at hand not only builds trust within our team, but also keeps them prepared to continue running the business when I'm not on site.

Communication may be a major key, but sometimes not even that can prepare anyone for the hectic life that comes with being a mompreneur. I married the love of my life in 2014 and in 2016 I became pregnant with my baby girl. Now there I was a newlywed, raising a family, investing in real estate (yeah I do that too), running Medical Solutions Academy and dealing with my body changing due to pregnancy on a daily basis. Did I mention I was acting as the office manager, because I was in the process of finding someone reliable to hire. Yeah, being a mompreneur can be hectic. I had my beautiful daughter on September 14th via cesarean delivery, which was totally unexpected. At this point I was in severe pain and had to allow someone with only one week of training to operate my business. Talk about stressful! I worked from the hospital bed when my baby girl was only a day old. We have to do what we have to do.

I occasionally miss family functions due to my schedule at times; however, I try to keep these instances to a minimum. They say it takes a village to raise a child, and luckily I have just that for both of my children. My mom has been my anchor especially when it was just me and KeShaun, taking off work whenever I needed her to be there with him so I could work. My family and friends have also been supportive and willing to step in if I could not be there. Luckily, I now have a loving husband who is there to take care of both kids and help more in the home when I need to be away at work.

For the most part everyone in my family is understanding of the demands of my business, but I can always tell when someone, especially a child, needs a little extra attention. They become a little clingy like only people who love you can do. I try to make a conscious effort to set aside special time for both my husband and son so they can feel loved and appreciated. We will all watch movies together and I spend separate one on one time with them as well. I often find myself simply lying in KeShaun's bed with him, even if it's just to watch him play video games. One of the most intimate moments of my day is that quality time spent with my family, interacting about the day's events or just having random talks. Family is very important to me and I like to show them in action, not just words.

Even though I do my best to make my loved ones feel appreciated I still sometimes feel inadequate despite my efforts. I constantly wonder if I'm spending enough time with everyone in my life, mostly Terrel and KeShaun since Madison is constantly tied to my hip. Sometimes I even wonder if I'm spending enough time by myself. One thing I do ensure is that I get the required rest that I need. If I am not properly rested, I cannot perform up to par and am of no use to anyone. Aside from getting rest, I know I could dedicate more time to taking care of myself. I'm constantly working to change that.

It's been nine years since I've had an infant; I had forgotten how demanding babies can be. My little girl is such a blessing, but she leaves me physically drained at times. Like most mothers I cannot help but spoil her. She is always full of smiles and joy and she has become the highlight of my calls and meetings with the staff. She is a good baby that does not fuss much, but working with her at my side is still challenging. However, being there to watch her firsts in everything and to see my son walk through the door everyday after school makes it all worthwhile. Because of the freedom entrepreneurship awarded me, I have had the opportunity to be home with my son daily when he gets home from school. Now I am blessed to be home with my daughter daily.

Every mompreneur faces the fear of whether she's balancing everything correctly, but she wouldn't be a mompreneur if she didn't push forward despite that fear! We may not realize it, but when family loves you, they will always support you. No one is perfect and beating yourself up when you feel like you've missed the mark will only cause a downward spiral. Who made "the mark" anyway? If you're giving your best each day, that's all anyone can ask of you. And your best will change each day with how you feel. Don't get discouraged by your shortcomings, just pick up and start over again the next day. I remind myself that I am doing the best I can and everything I do is for the betterment of my family, as I intend to leave a legacy. I embrace the fact that everything great requires sacrifice.

Just to help myself feel better about what I've accomplished day to day, I keep tabs on every task I need to do then check off what I've accomplished for the day. I am still old fashioned, using pen and paper to write out to-do lists and daily tasks. I keep an assortment of notebooks for lists and depend on my daily planner to maintain my schedule as well as my family's schedule. I also bought my son a weekly planner to teach him to maintain his own schedule. With him keeping notes of his own tasks I don't have to remember as he is sure to remind me of his upcoming tasks and events. This also teaches him responsibility and hones his organizational skills. It can become a bit much making sure everyone is doing what they are supposed to do, but having a family who takes authority over their own schedules can lessen the load.

Owning my business and calling the shots allows me to instill entrepreneurship values into my son. I talk to him in detail about the in's and out's of business and focus on the benefits of entrepreneurship to make his dream come true versus working for someone else. I often use examples from different business situations and relate them to real-life in a way he can comprehend. This method also makes him a little more empathetic when duty calls at work. He understands that mommy is doing this to give him and his sister a better future.

Looking into my children's eyes motivates me daily and makes me grind it out even on the days I am just not feeling it. Oh, you thought because I was a mompreneur those days don't hit me too? We are all human; anyone who says they don't have those days is lying to you. I also said previously that it's what you do to push past those feelings of inactivity and idleness that take you to the next level. Remember we all have our days, but we must give our best with each day anew. It was in those moments where I pushed myself harder that I found the inspiration for Dream ChasHers. I wanted to inspire the new entrepreneur or fellow mompreneurs to let them know it could be done. I didn't have guidance when I started my business, so I created the forum I would have liked when I started.

I know there are so many mothers out there who want to start their own business but don't know where to start. My first piece of advice is just to start. There's no other way to do what you want other than to simply go for it. Trust me when I say your kids will thank you later. You don't want to look back on your life and still have that business idea in your mind that you never pursued, or even worse watch someone live out the dream you never followed. Leave the "what ifs "behind, and go for it. Imagine if we all used our children as the reason why we didn't pursue our dreams. If every mother used that as an excuse, there wouldn't be any mompreneurs.

Use other women as an inspiration and know that you are capable of just as much as anyone else. You might have to fit more into your daily schedule, lose some sleep in the beginning, and even sacrifice some time; but in the end it's all worth it. I haven't punched a clock in over five years and I am not looking back!

It also helps to have a supportive family and work team so you don't have to carry the bulk of the weight alone. I am lucky enough to have a husband who backs my decisions and trusts my instincts. He understands that I only want what is best for our family so he meets me in giving 100% to make that happen.

Patience and resilience are essential to being a good mom and a good entrepreneur. We all face our share of blows with both and often plans are altered and expectations are not met; but you have to take those blows as they come and keep going. Every mom knows what it is to have grit and keep pushing when you don't feel like it. Think about all the times you had a sick baby or child, but you still had to go to work the next day and arrange a sitter because you couldn't miss any days on your 9-5 job. At least you now have the convenience to be able to call the shots if needed; you just also need to be prepared to put in the extra work that comes with being the boss. I swear when my alarm goes off in the morning, I just want to scream! Once I get up and moving though, I'm a force to be reckoned with! Try to change your perspective and see the positives in being a mompreneur. Hey, you could always go back to that 9-5 and answer to someone else again!

One of the most important realizations you can have as a mompreneur is the understanding that things are constantly going to change. All you can do is change with them. I am constantly thinking of new ways to potentially make life easier on both ends of the spectrum. There are always better ways to manage time, so I just find the optimal methods that work for me and my family. I can multi-task like no other, answering business emails while feeding Madison or lying in KeShaun's bed while he plays the game and I work on assignments. Of course, I feel like a crazy lady at times, but I would not have it any other way! Now that I have my own business, my kids are never far away from me. I look at it as a blessing to instill business principles in them at such an early stage in life, and have strong faith they will follow in my footsteps in their own adulthood.

Whoever made up the rule that women can or should only do one thing at a time had to be a man! I think people forget how strong mothers are, and sometimes we allow the world to make us forget too. Being a mom comes with so many constantly changing emotions; sometimes it's easy and sometimes it's the most difficult thing ever. When you add being an entrepreneur to that life, you have a complete madhouse! But listen to this... You do not have to do everything all the time. There will be some failure along the way, but it's all part of the process. Give yourself enough grace to allow room for failure and get back up and keep trying no matter what.

If you can control the way your mind thinks of being a mompreneur, I strongly believe you will make it through the process. Too often we allow self-doubt and fear creep into our minds and gain control of our thoughts. All of a sudden what once seemed easy now seems impossible all because of negative thinking. We are our own biggest enemy in life. Next thing you know, you're convincing yourself not to quit your job and go into business for yourself because you don't want to have to sacrifice time with your family (like you're not already doing that at your 9-5). If you focus on what could go wrong instead of all the things that are going right, then everything will fall apart quicker than you could ever imagine. You have to have faith in yourself and on the days you can't put faith in yourself, put it in God because there is absolutely nothing he cannot do.

What is meant for you is for you and no one can deter you from receiving your blessings.

Being a mom does not mean you cannot go after your dreams; in fact, it should make you go harder. Every day brings a new challenge that only a mom could tackle; being a mom comes with a skill set that will make handling business seem like a cake walk when you've set your mind to achieve the vision. Instead of seeing motherhood as a hindrance from entrepreneurship, think of it as a way to be a living example to your kids. If you believe in your dream, keep pushing! With everything going on, I sometimes feel like I'm swimming with my head barely surfacing the water; however, I make it a point to always stay focused and keep my eye on the prize! I have my days where I get in my corner and cry. Believe me, crying is perfectly normal! But don't stay in a pity party; instead, you have to get back up and go after what is yours! It will all work together for your good as long as your intentions are pure and you put in the work. Dreams don't work unless you do! So go ahead my fellow mompreneur and chase those dreams.

ABOUT THE AUTHOR

Mrs. Lakesha Reed-Curtis, wife and mother of two, is a woman of action who Dreams Big and just decided to Chase Hers! She was born and raised in Danville, Virginia, but now currently resides in Charlotte, North Carolina with her loving family. Her focus in life has always been to find different avenues with the opportunity to provide services to the community. Her goal then became to provide higher education opportunities for students interested in the healthcare field to advance career wise in the future. By introducing Medical Solutions Academy to her community, she has become dedicated to empowering her community through educational programs that serve to make prospective health care workers prepared for employment in the medical field.

Lakesha Curtis has fourteen years of hands-on nursing experience and received both her Bachelor and Master degree from Winston-Salem State University. By establishing Medical Solutions Academy, she has gained adequate experience in the full process of operating and administrating successful medical certification programs from start to finish. She has had the opportunity to witness students complete these certification programs over the course of the last six years. Her educational program has expanded over the years and now includes Nurse Aide, Phlebotomy Technician, Pharmacy Technician, Medical Assistant, Medication Aide, Medical Office Assistant, CPR Certification, and soon LPN. She has built this school from the ground up and enjoys playing such an important role in others' lives.

    Constantly facing the demands of maintaining a family and a career simultaneously, Lakesha understood how difficult it is for some women to chase their own dreams. She saw the need to form a group of empowering women to keep each other motivated, which sparked the beginning of Dream ChasHers. She now hosts weekly phone calls with this group where she is coordinator of the discussions and even held a vision board party to kick of the new year. She plans to host even more events in the future and build Dream ChasHers into another one of her empires. Although she may wear many titles, she wears them all effectively and efficiently while encouraging other women that they have the power to do the same.

Dreamchashers.com
info@dreamchashers.com
Instagram @lakesha_curtis , @dream_chashers, @medicalsolutionsacademy
Facebook: Facebook.com/lakeshareed

Chapter Five

Raising Businesses & Babies
By: Lenise R. Williams, Esq.

"I can have it all. I can manage it all," she said.

"It is impossible. There is no way you can be partner at a law firm, work the required long hours AND be a mom that is home in time to cook dinner and tuck everyone in bed," my male law school classmate (and boyfriend) said sternly to another classmate

As I sat there and listened to the two of them debate during a study session in the library, I realized that I was torn. As a single woman without kids, I hadn't really given much thought to children and how they would fit into my law career and future plans. *"Was it possible to have it all... Was this guy right? Would a mom really have to sacrifice?"* The two of them each made valid points during their discussion and it made me think about what I *really* wanted in my future personal and professional life.

Three years later while sitting in a Law Office Management class- which I took only because I thought it would be an easy 'A'- I found myself intrigued by my professor and her lifestyle. She drove a few hours from her hometown every Friday to teach this class. She spoke about her experiences, her wins and her losses and how she had so much freedom to do whatever she would like. She was very different from the other professors at the school. *"Was this for me? Did I want to have my own practice? Would I be successful?"* I hadn't seen myself as a business owner before. Although I knew

I wanted to be successful as an attorney I really hadn't considered the path I would take to get there.

One year after that class, two years after that heated discussion during the study session and just two weeks after graduating from law school, I found out I was pregnant. I did not think that I had a maternal bone in my body. While many girls grow up with the hope and excitement of being a mother, I had none of that. As a matter of fact I didn't even like to play with baby dolls as a child. The entire time I was pregnant I doubted my capabilities of being a mother. I wondered if I would be patient, if I'd be overly stressed by the sound of a baby crying or if I'd really be able to connect with a child. I was nervous and like many others that knew me, a little in disbelief. "A baby? You're having a baby? I never would have imagined!", said a college friend that I ran into when I was 8 months pregnant shopping for baby clothes.

The day my first son was born and I saw his face for the first time all of the anxiety was gone. Every book I read, every mom I drilled with questions was right- once I saw him I was instantly in love. I loved him so much that five months later when I started working, I would use my lunch break to leave the office and visit him at his daycare. Being a mom became the most important thing.

I worked for about six weeks at a firm and resigned; it wasn't the right fit for me. My classmate (that was now my fiancé) was right; it was not the ideal job that allowed for lots of quality time with children. Eventually after withstanding some peaks and valleys (you can read more about that in my book *She Conquered*) I became an entrepreneur- I opened my own law firm.

I appreciated this experience. Although it was stressful not knowing if I'd make enough money to pay the office rent some months, it was worth it. I realized how advantageous it was when my son had his first performance as a Pre-K student. I cleared my schedule and showed up in the middle of the day to sit on the front row with my camera in hand. I am proud to say that after 13 years of entrepreneurship and the addition of another son, I have not missed much. As a divorced parent I have to make it a priority to be there- I don't want them to ever look into an audience or a stand full of fans and not see one of their parent's face. They deserve that.

The practice of law is stressful. In a practice in which I worked on mainly criminal and domestic matters, I became emotionally numb to many of the issues. During this time I also went through a divorce and became a single mom to my two young boys. This added to the stress and created more of an emotional drain.

Despite the stress and my mental/emotional state, I had to keep going. For the most part I was able to control my schedule. On some days when I had scheduled court appearances I was unable to control my day; I had to be there. As my caseload got heavier those days in the courtroom increased. I found myself waking up earlier, getting the kids to daycare, working all day nonstop, picking them up from daycare (typically they were one of the last to be picked up), getting home, feeding them, bathing them, putting them to bed and then pretty much passing out from exhaustion. I was spending the day helping many people fix their problems (criminal and domestic), but I was creating my own because I wasn't the mother my boys deserved. I was cranky, irritable and on edge all the time.

I remember thinking:
"This cant be my life. There has to be more."

There is something about the emotions that a divorce will provide. For some it puts them in a bad place; a place of darkness and sadness. Eventually I allowed the emotions to help me evaluate myself and what makes me happy. In this experience I realized what was important to me and what was not. My conclusion was simple: my happiness, my children and my children's happiness were the only things that were truly of importance. Through prayer, support from family and friends, lots of self-help books and some alone time on the weekends that my ex husband had our kids, I finally decided to take that leap to discover how to incorporate all the things that were important. Of course money was important- I needed it to eat and to take care of the kids. I mean, food IS essential for our happiness (and health)! However, maybe a large amount of money wasn't as important. I was trading my time for money. I thought that maybe I could simply reduce the time.

I started to recognize that there were so many ways that I could work smarter and not harder. I began to incorporate more technology in my practice. I had appointments only on certain days of the week, I reduced the amount of domestic cases I accepted (those were the most draining) and I had my legal secretary scanning and sending more documents to me via email so that I could work outside of the office. I also started to look into other ventures that required less of my time, yet still yielded a good return. I recognized that it was possible to make a great salary outside of the legal profession doing things that I loved. Eventually I stepped away from my law offices- I had two in two cities. I wanted more businesses in which I did not have to trade so much time for dollars! I went after just that.

During this time my youngest son gave daycare providers the blues! I had been asked by several providers to remove him from their school. At times it was really hard for me to work because I was constantly getting calls from the daycare regarding his behavior. It was such a rough time in my life and I hated the way the providers treated me. Also as a mom that was fortunate enough to spend lots of time with my eldest child as a baby/toddler, I knew how much those little minds were capable of absorbing. I hadn't found a daycare that could fit my youngest child's needs nor provide the type of accelerated learning I could give at home. For this reason my first full time business after the law practice was a Christian early learning center and preschool. I couldn't find what I wanted so I created it.

Despite naysayers telling me that a lawyer couldn't run a daycare, I did it anyway. Once I got the keys to the facility I had my children (at this time ages 4 and 6) helping me paint the walls, pick out new toys, haul the trash and more. They proudly wore t-shirts representing the school and loved telling everyone that I was the owner. Eventually things went south between the building owner (former owner of the school) and myself and I decided to walk away.

Walking away from that venture was one of the hardest business decisions I've had to make. I invested enough money in the business to send my children to college and was emotionally vested in not just the business, but also the families the school served. I was devastated. However, in business you have to know when to push and know when to cut your losses. Some called it failure. However, I called it lessons. I took over a preschool with less than 20 children enrolled full time and in less than two years had it near capacity. I increased enrollment tremendously, implemented a real curriculum and brought life into a business that was otherwise doomed. That, in my opinion, was not failure.

When you know for whom you are making all you decisions, it becomes easy to decide.

The business was still costing me money- it was just about at the break-even point when I decided to cut my losses. Although I had invested so much money I was still putting money into it each and every week. Parents were late paying tuition that I needed for payroll- guess who had to pay it. Yes, ME! The stress from the landlord combined with the financial strain caused me to say goodbye. I was ensuring that all the children in the school were fed, but what about my own? As a single mom I made the best decision. I chose my kids.

Of course I did not stop after that; it is just not in my nature. I moved on to other business ventures that did not require so much capital- I learned my lesson! Each venture my boys were right there. They have been my cheerleaders, my secretaries, my runners and more.

There was a time that I was fed up with the school system and I withdrew both of my children from elementary school. I did not take a year to plan and find all the resources like most families do before homeschooling. I woke up one morning and decided that was what I wanted to do and by 4pm that day I withdrew them. Being an entrepreneur gave me the luxury to do just that. I did not have to worry about who would care for them while I was working. I did not worry about who would outline their assignments. I had the freedom to be home with them and arrange meetings around my babysitter's schedule. I woke up a few hours early everyday to outline their work for the day before they got out of bed. They not only had their school work for the day, but being home with me gave them life/business lessons as well.

By this point I was offering consulting services for entrepreneurs. My children would sit on the floor and listen to my phone conversations between me and my clients. After getting off a call I remember my son once saying, "Mom, that lady's business didn't sound like a good idea. How will she make money from that?!" It was funny because he read my mind; that was my same thought! It was at that moment that I knew that they understood. All the years of toting them to business meetings, introducing them to my new ventures- it was now worth more than all the money I ever lost in any venture.

It is worth so much because I have successfully changed the generations to come. I did not grow up rich nor did I come from a family of successful entrepreneurs and influencers. I came from a hard working family that consisted of most family members working paycheck to paycheck. I grew up thinking that my life would be the same way. I thought that I'd be lucky to make $40,000 per year as a first generation college kid and live in a decent neighborhood, come home and cook dinner every night, become stressed over motherhood and get up the next morning for the next 40 years to go to the same job. That was the American dream, right? Having a successful business, having the freedom to travel, enjoying time with kids, driving really expensive cars, affording the very best schools- that was all for lucky people not regular people like me.

Along that "happy" journey I started over ten years ago after my divorce I read so many books and met so many people that helped to change my mindset. I realized that those things weren't for "lucky" people. Those things were available to every "regular" person that worked hard (and smart) enough to get it. I studied successful people. I looked at what they accomplished and searched the internet to read their stories of how they accomplished such amazing things. Success can always be duplicated. We do not have to reinvent the wheel; it just requires an idea and tracing the path that many others have taken. Of course they all had a testimony; every successful person does. They all also had a different mindset than the one I had for over 30 years. Changing my mindset was not only beneficial to me, but also beneficial to my children.

My children don't just say that they can do and be whatever they want in life; they one hundred and ten percent believe it. I have two of the most confident and intelligent children. It is not because I write motivational quotes or have them repeat affirmations every morning. They are that way because of the things and people that I have exposed them to. Please do not think this was my plan all along. I was really just learning more about success, mindset and happiness and it inadvertently rubbed off on them. I am so happy that it did.

The direction that the world is headed right now, more and more jobs are being done away with. Social media marketing, online businesses, YouTube success stories are all making competition that much harder. People need to know how business works even if they have no desire of entering entrepreneurship. They need to understand it just in case one day they are pushed into entrepreneurship just to survive. I did not sit down and teach my children anything about business and how to make their own money. A child learns what is right and wrong, positive and negative, etc. simply from watching. If they are in a negative environment it becomes the norm. The same is true if they grow up around business, taking nice vacations, caring about others, being encouraged to read- that all becomes the norm and that is what they aspire to have/do later in life.

These two little boys can talk about business with grown ups. They can talk about margins, valuations, copyright, trademark, marketing- the whole nine yards. My son recently asked me for $200 to buy sneakers. Now that he is in men's sizes and the price has increased, I told him that he needed to create a way to earn money. His challenge was to create a business that would not only earn money, but it would also help others. He came up with such an amazing business model! Because I am his lawyer (smile) and as of the printing of this book we have not protected his intellectual property I cannot share. However, if you continue to follow me and my journey you will soon learn more about it.

My youngest son, the more outspoken/outgoing of the pair, loves to tell everyone about the things that I am working on. He tells his friends, his teachers and anyone else that will listen. Sometimes I have to tell him to be quiet and not tell everyone everything about me. He gives out business cards, tells people my website, comes to business events that I host and is so proud to tell everyone that he is my son. Not only are my boys proud of me, but I am also so proud of them and the amazing things that I know they will accomplish.

One of the best pieces of advice was given to me when I was going through my divorce. I remember telling a friend that now that I was a single mom of two young children, I could not do all the things that I wanted to do. I couldn't go out to nice restaurants, I couldn't go on great vacations, I could not take the quick road trips that I enjoyed so much to visit friends. Her response was simple. "Yes, you can. Take them with you and they will adapt." That one simple piece of advice changed things for me ten years ago. It did not only apply to my personal life, but I made it apply to my business as well. Moms have to eliminate the thought that they cannot start or grow a business, go to a meeting, etc because of their kids. Kids will adapt only because they will not have a choice! Sitting in a waiting room while I have a quick appointment, being very quiet while I am on a business call, sitting on the floor under my desk while I am typing a proposal- those thing have become the norm.

Whatever was possible before kids is possible after! It may take longer days and shorter nights, juggling multiple things like a circus clown, but through it all everyone can achieve business, babies and balance.

ABOUT THE AUTHOR:

Lenise Williams is an advocate for entrepreneurship. Not only is she an advocate, she is also an Intellectual Property Attorney and Business Strategist. She works with existing businesses to develop more profitable brands and assure that a brand's intellectual property (trademark, copyright, patent) is protected. Although she has an extensive list of training and degrees, her expertise is also from personal experiences as a serial entrepreneur owning and operating multiple businesses for nearly 15 years.

In order to fulfill her goal to encourage entrepreneurship and women in leadership positions, Lenise travels hosting seminars and public speaking. Lenise has spoken to small groups of college students to gracing international stages such as the United Nations 2016 Conference in Marrakech, Morocco and Hive Global Leaders Program in Africa. In addition Lenise has worked with large companies such as Home Depot and Zaxby's Chicken franchise to companies with only member. She is also the founder of Girl Biz Academy, an organization designed to teach female middle school- college age students entrepreneurial and leadership skills. Additionally she volunteers with The Launch Pad, a transition program for women overcoming homelessness. Lenise provides monthly business and leadership coaching to the ladies in the program.

Lenise is the author of the books "31 Day Guide to Building a Personal Brand", "She Conquered" and "Business, Babies, Balance: Real Stories of Mompreneurs". Lenise uses her platform and her books as a means to help others find the freedom she has found through entrepreneurship.

Lenise and her two sons, Marcus age 12 and Evan age 9, reside in Atlanta, GA.

LeniseWilliams.com
info@LeniseWilliams.com
Facebook: facebook.com/momprenueresq
Instagram: @Mompreneur_Esq
Twitter: @MompreneurEsq

Chapter Six

Heart of a Mompreneur
By: Arleigh Hatcher, R.N.

"WERK..."

I have always wanted to be the boss. Whether on the playground, at school, at work, wherever. I wanted to be the person making the rules and living life the way I saw fit. When I was 24 years old I thought I was doing it too. The key word there is "thought." At the time I was a traveling registered nurse. I worked three days a week and switched hospitals and cities every three months. I had just gotten married and life was all good for me.

One day while I was at work, I could not for the life of me stay awake. I tried everything: standing up, turning on music, walking around; it seemed that nothing was working. Luckily, I had a desk job in a doctor's office with minimal patient contact at the time. There was something that was just off about the way I felt. I had a feeling that something incredible was going on. I hurried to the store as soon as I got off work and bought three pregnancy tests. The tests were from the dollar store (don't judge; that's what they use in the Emergency Room anyway). I didn't say a word to my husband about the possibility of us expecting. He is the excited type and I didn't want him to be disappointed if we weren't in fact expecting. When the first test came back positive I couldn't believe it. Then the second and the third tests all showed those two pink lines! All of them were positive and to say the least- my husband and I were overjoyed. We literally could not have been happier. Everyone that we shared the news with were incredibly excited as well.

My pregnancy was really "cute" initially. My only side effect was being sleepy. Then the sickness started: constant nausea, vomiting, and many other "fun" activities that come along with pregnancy. Being so ill caused me to miss time from work, which caused a drastic decrease in income. On top of that, my travel nurse status did not allow me to accrue paid leave time. Now, in addition to all the "fun" from the pregnancy, I also had to worry how long I could actually remain off from work after the birth. That time in my life was when I realized that there was so much more that I could do to earn a steady income while still having free time for my growing family.

I began to research ways that I could become my own boss, but I had some hard criteria to fulfill. I knew that whatever the eventual plan would be, it had to please God, serve the community, and somehow incorporate my nursing background. I wanted to be a woman who could spend time with her family while earning more than enough income to support myself. The first initiative that I took was to pick up a book similar to the one you are reading now. It was a series of stories about nurses who had taken a leap of faith to start their businesses. There were nurses who founded home care agencies, travel agencies, CPR training companies, consulting companies, and much more. I was amazed at their courage and I felt that if they could do it, surely I could too!

Initially, I was not ready to let go of my job so I decided to establish a part time business with room for growth. The very next day as I was browsing through the course offerings from my hospital, a CPR instructor course popped up. In order to attend all I needed to do was sign up and order the required books. That was such a blessing, and the timing could not have worked out any better. I am a firm believer that God puts you right where you need to be, right when you need to be there. Who knew that my path to full-time entrepreneurship would start with that $30 investment back in 2009?!

As soon as I completed the two-day instructor course, I was ready to get started on my new adventure. The first thing I did was get my business license from my local court house. Since it was a home based business I just used my county of residence. The process was very easy and not expensive at all. I would advise you to research what kind of business structure will work best for your business (Sole proprietorship, Partnership, LLC, S Corp, Non Profit, etc.) so that you can avoid some challenges that I had once revenue started to increase.

My next step was to find a website template company that would allow me to build a professional website that fit my business budget. I ended up building my site for $9.99/month, and I added the extra feature for $5 per month that placed me higher in local Google searches. Thankfully, our reliable internet was able to give me the tools that I needed to project a professional and experienced online brand.

In the beginning my business wasn't really busy at all.

In my entire first year I only made $5,000 in profit teaching CPR. At the time I was very proud of that because that money was in addition to my nursing salary. It was generated by my very own business and I was proud to call myself an entrepreneur with some actual profits no matter how small. For many people an extra $5,000 is great; heck, for me that was incredible. The problem with the amount was that it did not match the amount of time that I worked. You see, I was always busy. I was working full time, teaching CPR on all of my days off, and spending the rest of my small amount of time with my husband and my one-year-old daughter. $5,000 did not match the large amount of time I spent on the business and away from my family. I recall in the beginning driving an hour to teach one CPR and First Aid class for only $100. I quickly realized that my time was just as valuable as the customers. No matter if I had one person or 20 people, my courses took the same amount of time to teach. I could either make 1x the course fee or 20x the course fee. I chose the latter so that I could maximize my time and my profits. My time is much more valuable than money; setting limits is paramount.

Going into my second year, I made sure that my website clearly stated that I only came to business offices with at least five students. Otherwise, they had to come to me. The problem: I worked form home and did not have an office space for them to meet me. The practice of being a solopreneur/mompreneur working from home allowed me to build great relationships with my clients, but it completely stunted my business growth. My ultimate goal was always to spend more time with my family without having to sacrifice financially. Year two I realized it was time for me to hire some employees and find a home for Heart to Heart CPR. Year one I was a "one woman show". I was the web designer, marketer, instructor, manager, budgeter, and much more. The method of doing everything yourself can be necessary in the early days; however you will need a plan for growth. Delegating is essential so that you have a high quality of life.

Since I still worked full time as a nurse in a hospital, I had a pool of colleagues to look to as potential employees for my CPR company. I immediately sent out an email and got back a few responses from CPR instructors interested in making some extra money. I still remember how excited and nervous I was to have people actually working for me. I also recall the joy that I felt when I was at work one day and had two CPR classes going at one time that were taught by my two new employees. I was beginning to see my dream of leaving my full-time job unfold, but I was still in need of an affordable office space. At the time, I was leery of renting a space since CPR classes would come in waves; it was not consistent. While I am a risk-taker, the thought of adding the extra expense and the possibility of negatively affecting my family made me nervous.

For months I searched for rental spaces; nothing appeared to be the right fit for Heart to Heart CPR. I was so close to giving up my dream, but then something incredible happened. One October day in 2011 as I was driving to the grocery store something guided me to check out a building that was a bit off my route. I pulled up to the building and decided to go inside. The building manager happened to be available and showed me a few office spaces. The space was absolutely perfect, but the rent was much more than I wanted to pay. I declined and left the building feeling as though maybe I should just be satisfied with my current situation: I had two employees that helped with CPR classes that I would have typically taught on my days off and I was making extra money.

    One thing that I have learned is just to let God lead the way in all things. I have found that when I force things and stress, not much happens. However, as soon as I get out of the way God steps in and shows me that he had a plan for it ALL.

    December 2011 God stepped in. I received a phone call from the building manager of the space that I loved. The building manager told me that he believed in the service that I was offering the community and that he wanted to help in any way that he could. He said the mission of the building was to do God's work by helping people who want to help people. He then provided me with an offer that was perfect for my company. He offered the space for half of the initially quoted amount with free use of all of the conference rooms. I accepted right away and moved in the very next month.

Trust Yourself

Once I moved in I quickly found that my business doubled by just having an office for my clients to come. Having an office space worked positively for my service based business. Although many successful companies are able to operate from home, mine just didn't work out that way. As I continued to work full-time and book CPR classes, I began to gain confidence in being an actual business owner. It felt good to be able to contribute to my family and to help the community with a lifesaving skill.

After about six months in my new office my business began to supplement my income. I was able to reduce the number of hours I was working as an RN in the hospital and give my business more attention. While I was thankful for the growth, I still felt that I could be doing more. I felt like something was missing. This is a feeling that I have always possessed regardless of what I am working on. I always feel as if I can be doing something more.

In my quest to do more, I started to research other courses that I could offer as a Registered Nurse. I was surprised to find a wide variety of choices. My first addition was a Medication Aide and Pharmacy Technician Training program. Those first two courses created many long nights for me. I was very detailed-oriented and meticulous in creating the courses. I knew that it had to be a high quality program. However, all the long nights and lack of sleep paid off. It was all worth it!

My first Medication Aide class had five students and I was so proud! I was able to work even fewer hours at the hospital (only working three days per month) to free up the time to teach. Upon the start of my first Pharmacy Tech course, I hired another instructor to teach that class. I was blessed to have a flurry of students enroll for the class. After the start of that class I then had five streams of income: my job at the hospital, Medication Aide courses, CPR training, and Pharmacy Technician training and I also added a Nurse Aide training program. I was doing pretty well and within four months I was earning more than my salary at the hospital, but I still did not have the confidence to resign.

I was still operating my business with myself, one Pharmacy Tech Instructor, and two CPR instructors. Heart to Heart CPR was beginning to take up the majority of my time and it was only going to get busier. People say that when God wants you to grow, He makes you uncomfortable. Well, I was squirming in my seat, couldn't keep still, pacing the room, and sweating missiles uncomfortable. Like I have learned about many new entrepreneurs, I was completely racked with feelings of inadequacy and failure in my young company. These concerns came mainly from inexperience and the overwhelm of having to figure it all out on my own. Finally, I took it to God for guidance on how to proceed. I prayed about it and went to bed on it.

While watching Beyoncé's HBO special " Life is but a

Dream," I was inspired to take that leap from an employee to a full time employer. I had already been leaning towards putting in my two weeks because the Nurse Aide class that I was starting was rapidly approaching. The only problem was that I had zero students, my Medication Aide class had graduated, the CPR had slowed down and if I quit my job prematurely I feared that I would put my family in a financial bind. On the other hand, what if the class filled and I earned a bad reputation of not being able to deliver the course because I lacked the time because I was still working? I had some serious decisions to make. In the meantime I drafted a two-week notice, printed it and just looked at it and wondered.

I will never forget Valentine's Day of 2013, my husband and I were at home because it was on a Thursday and he had to work that night. My daughter was asleep and I was up watching Beyoncé's HBO special sipping a glass of wine. There was a part where she jumped into the ocean from her yacht and said the most fitting thing for my situation. She said "In my hardest moments, where I thought, what am I doing, I'm not strong enough for this, I can't get through this, I'm not ready, I just have to say jump! Because, I know I'm gonna land in that water and swim back on the boat and I'm going to jump again and land in the water and swim back to the boat. I have to trust myself." That stuck with me because no matter what happened with my company I was still a seasoned Registered Nurse; if nothing else I had that to fall back on. That was enough for me to finally make that "jump." I hit the send button on the two week notice to my boss, worked my two weeks (at one day per week lol), and I never looked back.

My first few months without my RN income were not easy. My first Nurse Aide class had only two students. I decided to go forward with it because one student paid in full and she was so excited to start the class. The other student was sponsored by an agency, and I didn't get paid for two months! It was rough starting out, but with the spiritual and financial support of my husband, mother, and grandparents, I was able to make it through. My husband supported me 100% as he knew this was a temporary sacrifice that we were making in order to achieve a goal.

Some people don't like to talk about receiving monetary help in the beginning, but it is sometimes necessary when your business is just starting out. Just having someone reassure me and tell me that they believed in me was a good "payment" as well. Thankfully, eventually we gained more scholarship resources, my mentors were able to help steer me in the right direction and my company started turning around for the better. There would be no Heart to Heart Career Training Center without the support of my family. Taking that leap of faith helped me to learn just how supportive they all could be. Taking that leap of faith brought out a better side of me It brought out the more focused, responsible, and understanding aspect of my personality. The experience also helped to retrain my mind to focus more on long- term effects as opposed to just reacting.

I was 28 years old, running a business, juggling my home life and professional life and for the most part just trying to make it all work. The majority of my students were young women with children who were also doing their best to make it all work. I was able to relate to the students, which aided in creating lifetime bonds with many of them. Life can get so hard and I love being able to connect with people and help them get to the next level despite difficult circumstances. At the same time, experience has taught me that being equally firm and fair was an integral part of running a successful company.

In the four years since I decided to fully trust God and have full faith in His abilities, Heart to Heart CPR has become Heart to Heart Career Training Center. We have added Phlebotomy, EKG Technician, Dental Assistant, as well as a few online courses to our roster. I have also transitioned from teaching altogether so that I can focus more on the operations and continuing to grow my company. Praise God!

In August of 2014, I found out that we were expecting again. I was 30 years old and my husband and I were hoping for our little prince. I knew that this would be my last baby so I wanted to celebrate this pregnancy just as much as I did with my daughter. With my first pregnancy we did belly casts, maternity photos, a huge baby shower, 3D ultrasounds, Lamaze class, everything we could think of to celebrate our new arrival. Naturally, when I was pregnant for the second time, I wanted to do everything that I had done with my first pregnancy and more. We began searching for a central place that could do everything, but we couldn't find anything outside of a standard 3D Ultrasound studio that was out of town. We even had a gender reveal with our family to find out the gender of our new baby at our house. When we popped that big black balloon, our family sounded like the crowd at the Super bowl as the blue confetti exploded into the air! I still remember the joy that my husband and I felt to know that our precious boy was on the way.

Our search for a place that could meet all of our needs brought back a dream that I had back when I was pregnant with my daughter. At the time, I didn't have the capital nor a clue as to how to get started. I wanted to open a 3D Ultrasound studio that served as a one-stop shop for pregnant women. I dreamed of it having spa service, a section for childbirth education, and an artsy section where moms could get beautiful belly casts or belly paintings, and maybe even a photography studio. If you noticed I am easily satisfied with doing the absolute most. The decision to include my family in this venture was imperative so that the business would have all the support that it needed.

After researching the market, the number of births in my city, and local competition I felt more and more confident in getting started on my reignited idea. At the time, I was placed on a series of short bed rests due to the pregnancy. Once because I was having early contractions, and another time because I had a degenerating fibroid which caused the worst pain of my life, including childbirth. In case you are unfamiliar with the term "degenerating fibroid", it basically means that my pregnancy hormones caused a previously unnoticed fibroid to grow rapidly in size. Once the fibroid ran out of blood supply, it essentially died a slow painful death inside of my uterus. Thankfully my baby was safe during the process, but I was in too much pain to walk and I could barely get out of the bed. That may have been TMI (too much information), but without that downtime when my doctor required me to take time off from Heart to Heart Career Training Center, I would not have had the time to research the market so thoroughly and our beloved ultrasound studio and spa may not have been established.

God is working on us all the time; it's always about your perspective though. I could have spent that time on bedrest crying in the bed all day, but that was not my assignment. I trusted God to take care of my baby and me, so I knew that things would work out the way that He wanted it to, no matter what I wanted. I feel that way in every situation, and that is what allows me to deal with the amount of work and stress that comes with being the boss that I dreamed of becoming so many years ago.

I created a business plan on a standard business plan template website and called a family meeting with my husband, my mom, and my grandfather and presented them with my ideas. Thankfully, they were able to see my vision and were all on board. They've been supportive like that, all the time and for my entire life. Sadly, during my pregnancy my beloved grandmother "Gigi" was placed under hospice care and passed away after battling cancer off and on for 18 years. If she had been alive to see it, she would have been right there, front and center, supporting my ideas and encouraging me to simply "Go for it." She had always shown complete confidence in me. As a child, I recall overhearing her telling her company how smart I was; I was shocked to hear her say that because she mostly commented on my smart mouth during my younger years. Hearing those words come from her when she thought I wasn't listening did a lot for my self-confidence growing up. As a teenager, she and my mother were the ones that pushed me to follow their footsteps in becoming a Registered Nurse. My family supported me all the way through nursing school so that I didn't have to work while trying to study for 12 hours a day. Nursing school was not a game, and I took it very seriously knowing the sacrifices made for me to have a successful career. Because of them, I graduated on time and was a Registered Nurse at 19 years old. Words can't express that gratitude that I have for my family.

The name that we chose for our ultrasound studio is very special to us because it holds my grandmother's name, Carolyn. The English meaning for Carolyn is Joy, which was a perfect embodiment of the feeling that we wanted families to have when visiting our ultrasound studio. We decided on the name Peek of Joy 3D Ultrasound and Spa as a way to continuously honor my grandmother's incredible legacy. Starting our brand new ultrasound venture seemed almost impossible at first. We needed a building, an ultrasound machine, furniture, computers, massage equipment, classroom space, employees; we were starting from scratch. It was much different from my training center where I started off as the only employee and built it up over time. Our ultrasound studio had to start with all of the bells and whistles already in place.

In regards to how all of that got accomplished, it was a series of blood, sweat, tears, and miracles; but mostly God. We were planning to rent an office space, but somehow ended up buying the building for much cheaper. We were planning to rent the 3D Ultrasound machine, but we were presented with a deal that we couldn't refuse and ended up buying that too. It seemed that just when we thought we had hit a roadblock that we couldn't recover from, the doors would just open up and it would work itself out. I'm not saying it was easy, because God always moves in His time and not ours, but eventually it all worked out. We were able to have our grand opening when my son was only four weeks old. Today, Peek of Joy 3D Ultrasound and Spa offers 3D Ultrasounds, Belly Casts, Belly Painting, Prenatal Massages, Maternity Photos, Life casting, CPR classes, and Lamaze classes. It is a gem in our hometown of Williamsburg, VA and we are so very proud of that.

Starting on this entrepreneurial journey seven years ago has taught me so much about life, relationships, valuing my time, and dealing with people in general. The impact that it has already had on my daughter is worth every single sacrifice. She sees no limitations on what she can accomplish. She knows in her heart that she is capable of achieving anything that she sets her mind to and she is stunned when she hears that everyone does not think that way. My daughter's goal at seven years old, is to open a Non-Profit called Homeless Care. At Homeless care, she says that food, housing, and clothes will be free for the homeless and she feels that she should be able to start her company by the time she is a teenager. It fills me up that she intends only to work in a field doing something that she loves and her one stipulation is that she has to be the boss. I politely asked her if she wouldn't mind referring her clients to Heart to Heart Career Training Center to help them establish a career, and she promised that she would. That's my girl!

While my son is only a year old, I am grateful that he will grow up only seeing his parents as business owners. My prayer for him is that he follows his dreams, whatever they may be, without limitations. Even at only a year old, he has an intensity about him that will be able to take him anywhere that he wants to go in his life as long as it is channeled in the right direction. God, I love those babies. They are my "why" for everything that I do.

There were so many sacrifices in the beginning but, my husband and I being able to drop off and pick up our kids from school, attend every practice and game, and just be present when it counts (and it always counts), shows me that this whole grind makes perfect sense. It seems that no matter what obstacles come my way, there is always a tugging feeling in my spirit that says They. Can't. Stop. You. That feeling is what pushes me through; it guides me never to quit and to pray that people tell me "no" quickly so that I move on in order to receive my "yes" from the right person. Some days I wake up and decide that someone is going to say yes today, whether it's a customer at Heart to Heart CTC, a new Mom at Peek of Joy 3D, or at Wal-Mart. I'm expecting it and my day isn't complete until I get it. The work that my team and I have been putting in and the miracles that God continues to perform in my life give me all the reassurance that I need to keep moving forward. I know deep in my heart that "They can't stop me!" and that is the most important lesson of all.

ABOUT THE AUTHOR

Williamsburg, Virginia's own Arleigh Hatcher RN is a born and raised native of York County and proudly upholds her family legacy of contributing to her local community in many ways. Bred from a deep -rooted history of women who save lives, she followed the family profession of becoming a nurse but has evolved into so much more. As a wife and mother of two, Arleigh touches the lives of people of all backgrounds through her school Heart to Heart Career Training Center as well as her newest family business Peek of Joy 3D & Spa, both based in the city of Williamsburg. Instructing young aspiring professionals as well as experienced and mature students for the past seven years, her influence reaches far beyond the hands she shakes when she bestows upon them their certificates. Through her certification programs, these professionals go into our community, providing quality healthcare for our parents, grandparents, and young children in our hospitals, schools, doctors' offices and homes.

Arleigh's newest joint venture with her family touches the next generation of Williamsburg natives even from deep within the womb by offering a special experience for expecting families via 3D and 4D imaging. Fusing the classic style from her mother and grandparents with her "new-school" forward thinking, she innovates this corner of the maternity industry by also offering the families who visit their studio and spa many ways to immortalize such a special time period in their lives.

This wildly successful young entrepreneur has been invited to speak to and inspire other young women who are looking to combine their passion and talents to provide for their families by owning their own businesses. Email admin@hearttoheartctc.com for booking.

You can find her on social media:
Instagram-@theentreprenurse, @peekofjoy3d, and @hearttoheartctc
Facebook- Arleigh Hatcher
Snapchat- Loveleigh143

Chapter Seven

Mom in Chief
By: Toni Robinson

Unconditional

No one can prepare you for this journey. They can tell you stories, you can read a book about it, but you will never understand it until you are on your own journey. What journey am I referring to you may ask? Being a mommy. From the time you miss your cycle, feel that wave of morning sickness, see your lower abdomen expand, feel that first kick, to the time you hear that first cry, your world from that point on has been changed forever. While developing, the little human that took up residence in your body created something special at the same time. Possibly initiated by the rhythmic tune of your beating heart, you and this little human create an unbreakable bond that becomes stronger as time passes. If you ask me, they take a piece of your heart once they leave the residence of your belly. That little piece of heart they steal away, forms into a love that is only shared between the two of you. It is an unconditional love, a maternal love that will empower you to move mountains if necessary. I thought I knew love, because I had love all around me. I loved my family; I fell in love with my man. That maternal love though, *that* kind of love defies all prior understanding. I never knew love could be so strong, so selfless, so overpowering. It changed me. It refined me.

I am a very spiritual person and the bible has a major effect on how I live my life. It states that children are an inheritance from God and a reward from the womb. When you think of an Inheritance, you may think of owning something, or a possession being passed down to you. In essence that is what occurred when you were blessed with the gift of giving life. It is truly a miracle that we have been charged with. Not only is it a gift, it is also a weighty responsibility. We as parents are responsible for another human life to instill morals, virtues, and principles. They become our prized possessions. The outcome of their life depends on what we train them to be. So for me, I accepted this weighty task for what it is: a gift from my Creator. Doing a good job became my obsession as the maternal role meant everything. Can I fulfill this to the best of my ability? Can I really provide them with something I never practiced? Will I be a good mom? I don't know about anyone but myself when I say that having the task of being a mommy is the most important job you can have.

Family is everything. Growing up I didn't have much monetarily; all I remember is fun times with my family. Those memories I hold and cherish deeply as they molded me into the woman I am today. So I knew how important nurturing relationships were. I felt the love and got the attention that made me strong because mom was there. Even if it was only just her. We were her priority and that impacted me so much. So as I began to raise my children it was mandatory that I applied all I learned from my childhood experience. Being present and involved was a huge priority. Now, some may say, "we live in a world where you can't afford to stay at home". A career most of the time trumps family, because the family has to eat. Both parents have to work and if you want to survive you have to suck it up and just deal. Work until you can retire. Although that was a reality for me upon becoming a parent, I deemed it necessary to make my family priority and not the other way around. So the seed was planted to become a mompreneur.

Motherhood

The summer of 2005 was HOT! Heat waves were passing through like they were going out of style and I just wanted to die. Being nine months pregnant in the summer is not cute! Sweat was dripping down my back, off my butt and down my legs!! To top it off, I was pregnant and living in NYC –a place where no one held the door nor did anyone typically get up from their seat as a courtesy on public transportation. Let's just say I was over it and wanted to deliver my daughter sooner than later!

After two days of false alarms, 16 hours of labor, and an emergency c-section, my firstborn arrived. She was a good baby, greedy, but good. She was very alert and always the loudest in the nursery when it was time to eat. Breastfeeding was horrendous. All the baby magazines could not prepare me for the pain. The first night struggling to nurse, it hit me like a ton of bricks- WOW! I'm a mommy! I was no longer in charge of life, this baby was. So, the transition from being independent to now having to tend to every whim of my baby was tough. Now raise your hand if as a new mother you knew that you would never catch up on sleep for the rest of your life?! Well I clearly didn't get the memo. The sleepless nights ensued as I was nursing and adjusting to that newborn life. I wasn't prepared for what happened next: just a day before my daughter was scheduled to get her vaccinations, she got sick. She was hospitalized for 1 week due to a bacterial infection and I almost lost it! On one occasion they were poking her trying to get a vein for an IV and my husband and I were distraught as we watched. We felt helpless. I never thought I could feel so much pain and concern for a person. This just showed me how trying parenting could be. We got through it and my baby girl began to thrive and grow. I felt as though I was getting a hang of this mom thing. Getting my mommy routine down made me feel in control. The real test was at the end of leave when I had to return to work.

  It killed me to go back to work and be away from my baby. I took five months off of work, using all of my paid time off, thinking that it would be more than enough. Clearly I thought wrong; it wasn't nearly enough time. I felt like I didn't want to miss out on anything like her crawling or saying her first words. Going back to work thinking that I was going to miss out on her development made me so sad. Before I became a mommy I loved my career; after I became a mommy my feelings changed. This was really tough and eventually I began to feel a lot of resentment.

At the time I worked as a technician for the New York City Transit Authority. I was a field tech, so I went out on service calls for repairs. It is a fast paced, think on your toes kind of gig. I carried a heavy tool bag and I travelled to each call amongst the straphangers (that is what you call passengers that ride the train).There were about 200 employees in my department and at the time only five women. I didn't want to be noticed just for being female so I worked twice as hard as my male colleagues. I wanted to be known for being a great tech. You have to demand respect but not come off as unapproachable. I held my own and I left my mark. They would request me on calls because they knew I got the job done.

Everything was good until I got pregnant. Believe it or not, I worked out in the field until I was eight months pregnant. Yes riding the trains doing repairs! I did that! What was astonishing to me was that a big corporation like the New York Transit Authority with at the time 36,000 workers, they did not have maternity leave!! I was shocked. Since I was one of five no one had given birth before me. Two of the ladies were my age with no children and the others had older children they raised prior to working for the Transit Authority. I set the precedent, and they had absolutely no clue of how to handle my pregnancy. I opted to take FMLA which wiped out all my time I had accrued and I then took the rest of my leave without pay.

Following my leave, I begrudgingly went back to work knowing I did not have any available days to take off because my personal days had all been used. Fortunately, at the time my mom owned a daycare and was able to care for my baby. Upon my return to work, being a career mom tugged at me constantly; I would rush home to go get her. Breastfeeding was a feat. Being the only female in my department, and being on the road all day it made it very difficult for me to pump milk. There weren't any provisions for moms out in the field to pump and store milk. Because I was unable to pump, my milk supply decreased and I was unable to nurse. That caused even more guilt. From the time I had her until my first day back, I hadn't had a period because I was breastfeeding. My first month back after I could no longer breastfeed, my cycle started. I had 1 period, just one! I put emphasis on this statement for a reason!

I went through my inner struggles: feeling guilty for being at work, sad that I couldn't take a day off angry my milk supply was getting low. Soon thereafter I went to my six - month check up. While at my appointment I was discussing birth control options and my preferences with the nurse practitioner. She let me speak and then looked at me and said,

"Toni, you are pregnant."

I replied in total confusion and disbelief, "Excuse me. What?"

"You are pregnant," she said again in a mater of fact tone.

At that moment I wanted to scream and I was literally about to hyperventilate. I just went through the ordeal of having my first born, I was having all these inner struggles because of work and now to repeat it in the next year??! I left feeling dazed and confused and a little nervous to have the talk with hubby. Would he be happy? Would he feel stressed? What will he say? I mean, we had a six -month old baby for goodness sakes! That was a rough night; I did a lot of praying.

The year 2006 was a rough year for me. Pregnant, raising a toddler, working a strenuous job all while my husband and I worked opposite shifts was challenging. I know that there is always a light at the tunnel and I knew mine would shine one day soon. I wanted to think positive for the new baby's health. Other than sheer exhaustion I had a great pregnancy. I did not have any sick time so it was truly a blessing that all went well with my pregnancy. Can you believe that I worked full time until my ninth month of pregnancy. There should be an award for that!

After I took my leave and went back to work the second time, my wheels started turning. "This can't be my life", were my thoughts throughout the day. I felt that there had to be a better way. The following year we purchased a home in the neighboring state of New Jersey. My commute to work became long and even more exhausting. It became more evident that working from home and choosing the road of entrepreneurship was the way I wanted to live my life. So the journey began.

Can't Knock the Hustle

Initially it was the idea of working from home that became my goal. July 2007 I wrote down that I wanted to be my own boss so I that I could be there for my family. I looked at that paper everyday. Moving to another state away from my job made the goal so important to attain because the commute to and from work was torture. Having our babies in tow was a struggle in itself. My husband and I would wake up early, get the kids dressed, drive to my mom's house, drop the kids off and then head to work. We had long days. Leaving home at 6 am to get home sometimes at 7 or later in the evening became our norm. Some nights I would be so exhausted that I would unknowingly fall asleep while caring for the children. I would wake up to mascara, tic- tac- toe on my bed, powdered filled bathrooms and more. It was a crazy time! It got to the point where it just became too difficult. My husband and I decided to choose work schedules that allowed one of us to be home during the day in order to avoid having to commute with the children.

Although we switched our schedules I still felt that there had to be a better way. I joined a Multi level marketing business which sold supplementary health insurance. It was ok but I couldn't see myself making enough of an income to replace my salary from my job. I also tried working as an independent travel agent, but that did not offer the income I needed either. Disappointed but not defeated I looked for other ways to accomplish my goal. After trial and error I decided to take a break from seeking entrepreneur endeavors. I put a pause on my goals.

I shifted my focus back to my career and decided to attempt to get out of the field work and seek the more corporate side of the industry. I figured having a desk job would be less taxing on my body. I submitted my resume for promotions within the company and began the interview process. I was not offered any of the positions for which I interviewed; this was an eye opening experience. I felt incredibly dejected as nothing seemed to be going in my favor. I began to doubt myself. However, I began to notice the politics and allegiances that were present in the office. It became even more evident when a former colleague got a position for which he clearly was not qualified. Upon that realization, the self doubt faded quickly. I then got angry. Here I was trying to do better, so I thought, and a person's work performance wasn't even considered! Instead it was who you knew and how loyal you were to them. It was so insulting and so upsetting that I wanted to leave even more after my observation and discovery. It was now 2013 and I was fed up; I wanted out! I felt I had to prove to myself that I could be my own boss. The opportunity, didn't present itself until that springtime of that year.

I apathetically continued to go to work daily. One day that Spring while out in the field I reached for my cell phone as it rang. As I attempted to grab my phone, answer and put it to my ear, it went flying from my hand. I had that instant fear that went coursing through my body- that feeling that any smart phone owner has had a time or two! I picked up the phone and the entire front screen was shattered. This was the second time in a month. I took matters into my own hands. Like most techies, I have the urge to tinker with things and do everything dealing with electronics myself. I am a DIYer to the max. I decided to purchase the replacement screen and parts. I went on YouTube and I learned how to repair the phone myself. "How hard can this be?" I thought. I did it! I was hyped!

My colleague saw that my phone had been repaired and asked where I had gotten it done so quickly. With pride I told him I had done the repair. He was impressed mostly because he previously tried it, but was unable to complete because the parts were so small. He then asked if I could repair his daughter's phone. I did it and word got around quickly. At first it was a hobby I had gotten good at. One day I was on my way to drop a phone off to a friend and I came across a person I hadn't seen in awhile. When I told them that I do cellphone repairs, this person told me it was an inspiration to see women doing repairs. That "aha" moment was like lightning!!! I got home and immediately got a pen and paper to jot down my thoughts. "Finally, this could be it! This could be my way out!" I thought. Not only did I want to inspire other women, I wanted to defy the odds. I wanted to be that oxymoron of a typical repair guy. I wanted to be the sassy, fierce repair WOMAN! Geek squad but in heels! I knew what I wanted to pursue; I had a vision. The game plan was then put into motion.

The Process

The year 2013 was a year of change. I changed my thought process, I changed the direction of my life, and from that point on I think that mentally I became an entrepreneur. They say you become something in your mind before it comes to fruition and I believe that to be true. You have to believe and then you become. Since my clientele was building, I wanted to take the next step and become a legitimate business. I asked around and was referred to a business consultant who aided me in the startup phase. I then acquired my LLC, registered my company and obtained a business account. One thing I was told early on that stuck with me was to protect my company and make sure to keep my finances in order. Based upon that advice I searched for an accountant and a lawyer with whom I felt a connection business wise. At this stage I was like a sponge. I was hungry to find out about business management, branding, and how I can remain profitable as well as have longevity. I listened to webinars, I read books, I joined groups, and I asked a ton of questions. My hobby turned into a real business and I wanted to do things right. You may have all the intentions of doing everything right but the reality is, you have to brace yourself for things go wrong. Something I failed to do was create a structured business plan. The lack of a structured business plan hurt me because I underestimated expenditures that I could have avoided.

On my journey, I realized we are all bound to make mistakes. Mistakes create room for lessons, and those lessons help you to become stronger and wiser. As I pushed forward despite setbacks from time to time, it was amazing to watch my idea grow and flourish. I have a very strong work ethic. I am a "get it done by any means" type of person. Juggling work and supporting my growing business although tough, was a must. I couldn't see myself giving all my energy to a corporation and then not doing anything for myself. No matter what, always take time to work on your craft, build something for yourself, invest in you! So if any of you reading this have doubts that it can be done, I am here to tell you it can. It's a process. You must stick to it and persevere because it is worth it. Now for me, I live and worked in two different states. I lived in New Jersey and commuted to New York; my time was limited. I had to find a way to balance it all. Therefore steps I took from here had to be very strategic and calculated.

I created a schedule and I tried my best to stick to it. I dedicated my morning commute to only focus on my spirituality. I read my bible, meditated on its words and did additional studying that helped me to stay focused, gain insight and fine tune myself overall. This was a great way to start the morning daily. What was key to my business successfully being mobile was that I created a workflow I stuck to. I carried must have digital devices everywhere I went. My setup was legit. I carried my office in my backpack. This allowed me to conduct my business anywhere. I carried my iPad, which was dedicated as my payment terminal, along with my merchant swipe device to take credit cards. I also carried my laptop, writing journals, a wifi modem, and an extra power source to keep my devices charged. I always got to my job early, so I used that time to build brand awareness on my social media platforms. I found that my audience was very responsive in the morning, so I would engage at that time. Throughout the day, any breaks that I received at work I would use the time to respond to customer emails and return phone calls.

By the day's end I would go home or go do repairs. I had a lot of clients in New York, so I dedicated Tuesday and Friday only to field - work. My husband was very supportive when I went out to do repairs; he would watch the kids with no problem. By the end of the week I would check my mailbox at the post office to see if any mail in repairs were waiting for me to tackle over the weekend. This was my rhythm. I did this and began to see profit so I took my next steps.

I contemplated whether I should open a storefront or remain mobile. At first I thought it would be more logical to open a store. But as I thought about my circumstances and my end goal to be more present at home, a store didn't make sense for me. I began to think way outside of the box. I began to look more into unconventional methods of running a business and that is what led me to purchasing a work truck. Not just any truck though, a truck in which I could actually perform the work/repairs. I have an awesome family and they all played a part in helping me succeed. My sister and brother in law, found a great deal on a work van that was perfect for my vision, but the owners were in Delaware. My sister and brother in law knew I had to work and couldn't get off, so they took off of work, went to Delaware, checked the truck out, then took care of drawing up a contract and putting a down payment to hold it until I could pick it up and drive it home. I was overjoyed! The support was immense. When I got the truck home I was hyped! At the same time that this was going on, I was getting my name and logo trademarked, and having my lawyer find out all there is to know about a mobile service. I began to also price out what I needed to brand and work out of the truck. After all the work and effort, it was a frustrating moment as I learned there were zoning and other laws which would prevent me from operating the way I planned. Fortunately, it all worked out. My truck was on the road and people began to recognize the brand. My business evolved into something great, but the money just was not enough. After all of this it felt like I hit a brick wall.

Love it or Leave it Alone

I got to a point where I thought I had reached my potential with my business. I had no more ideas to flip and due to certain zoning laws in my area it made it a little harder to execute my great marketing ideas. Quite honestly I was stuck. I didn't know what else I could do. I was thinking of adding more services, but I didn't want to spread myself too thin. I never stopped learning and taking advice from those who had been down the same road I was traveling. So I invested in my business again and had a very impactful consultation. I traveled to Georgia in February 2016 for a day to meet with attorney/brand strategist Lenise Williams. The purpose for the visit was to create a plan of execution to create multiple streams of income for myself. She opened my eyes to a completely different outlook of my business. My process was completely revamped and I had a plan that would get me to my goal of retiring from my 9 to 5. I structured four pillars of ways to make residual income and really up the ante with my contributions to women in tech. So I hit the ground running.

When you know better you do better. I feel in my heart that when you learn something it is your duty to implement it in someway in your life. You have the responsibility to act upon it. I began to polish up my personal brand and worked on creating a strong digital presence. I then was prepared to go after contracts, offer consulting services, become a public speaker, and really represent women in tech. This paid off so well. I gave myself a year to really hone in on that plan, piece by piece until I executed everything. So once the structure was set, I could actually be in a position to become a fulltime entrepreneur. So I went from contemplating leaving the business to falling back in love with it. There is nothing that will jeopardize my family, so if at that moment I felt it wasn't going to grow into what I needed it to be financially, I would have left the idea. I would not have left the vision, but the idea of how I would become a mompreneur. I think it is vital to be realistic; to be honest with yourself as to whether what you are pursuing is even profitable. Asking, has it grown into a business, or is it a hobby or a side hustle in which you can supplement a small income? There is nothing wrong with going back to the drawing board. Everything worked out for me and it has been a blessing.

Is It Attainable?

As I write this I have stuck to my goal of a year to potentially leave my 9-5 job after 15 years. I still followed a process though. You can't just do things spontaneously when you have a family; other people are depending on you. I waited until I received a new batch of vacation and I was able to take 6 weeks vacation. This allowed me to take full advantage of testing my business out fully while still banking a check. In this time I have expanded and hired 3 people to take over and do my repairs. I now run a seamless operation in which I have developed a passive income. This has allowed me to be home more and be with the ones I care about the most. I now help others strategize and start their own mobile businesses. I've also created great digital products which also provide additional passive income. I've learned to package up the jewels that are in my brain and sell this knowledge. I've been invited as a keynote speaker representing women in tech as well as innovation in start-ups. I am a mompreneur- I am a business owner. This was all done while working a 9 to 5, living in another state and having two children.

If I can do it anyone can. If you yearn to be there for your kids and fit your work around your lifestyle instead of fitting your lifestyle around work, being a mompreneur is the answer. Analyze the skills you already have. How can you monetize off of what you have learned in the corporate world? Think outside of the box.

Always think of the skills you have and what problem you can solve utilizing those skills. Make smart strategic steps. Prepare your family for the experience and have an open line of communication with your mate. Always think objectively about a decision you will make, never while emotional. Get your credit in order. Start saving. Always surround yourself with people who have been through the journey or on the road with you. Always take time out of your day to work on your own stuff. Keep learning. Network and make purposeful connections. Never ever count yourself out. Take the leap!

ABOUT THE AUTHOR

Toni Robinson is a mompreneur in every sense of the word. Using her passion to be her own boss as well as her earnest desire to be present in her daughters' lives, she has harnessed all of her skills from her 15 year tech career to start her first business: Stilettos & Screwdrivers Mobile Electronic Repair Company. Her intention was to show her two daughters, young girls and other women that they not only have the capability to be a woman in the tech industry, but can also excel and not compromise their femininity. Her success in her mobile business endeavors has allowed her to start her own consulting company, T. Robinson Enterprises, which assists fellow techs in starting their own mobile businesses and help those already in business enhance their brands. She also is a public speaker, focusing on topics such as Turning Passion into Profit, How to Excel as a Woman in a Male Dominated Field, How STEM is Imperative in the Lives of All Youth, and How to be a Successful Mom In Chief. The highlight of her life as a serial entrepreneur is to be able to fit her work around her lifestyle and not fit her lifestyle around work.

For more information on Toni:
Stilettos-n-screwdrivers.com
Hello@stilettos-n-screwdrivers.com
Instagram: @stilettos_n_screwdrivers.com
Facebook: Stilettos & Screwdrivers LLC
Twitter: @hottechsns
LinkedIN: Toni Robinson

Chapter Eight

A Journey Worth Taking
By: Latanya Sanders-Kelker

Hello I am Tanya Sanders-Kelker. I am a wife and mother to three boys; yes that's right I'm a "Boy Mom". I am a collector of memories over material things, an impulse traveler, lover of spending time with my husband and kids, part-time foodie, semi-pro home cook and on top of that I am the entrepreneurs' accountant. All while being an affectionate and domestic wife, active parent and involved church member; I was able to follow my dreams and passion to start my own accounting and finance firm where I help small to mid-size businesses, particularly in the beauty and services industries, increase their profits and grow their businesses. I am also a personal financial coach helping individuals change their mindsets about money in order to reposition them to become more financially fit.

I have owned my own accounting and financial firm for about seven years now. I like to say I was pushed into entrepreneurship because I know for a fact that I would not have jumped out there on my own; I needed a push. I always knew at some point that I would like to be my own boss and own my own business, I just never in a million years thought that I would have started my journey so young and so fast. How young and how fast you ask? Well immediately after obtaining my MBA in operational management and finance I secured a job that I really enjoyed. The position paid well, I loved my co-workers, I loved the owners and I genuinely loved what I was doing there. I was only there for a little over one year before they did a mass lay off, which included my position. I was devastated! I felt blind sighted, heart broken, and confused. I couldn't believe that I had been laid off. As a matter of fact I was downright scared because I didn't have a back up plan in place nor any idea of how I would be able to continue to survive.

I had just had my first son and I was a single mom at that time so I couldn't take time to wallow in my despair. I had to ensure my finances were in tact to continue to provide for myself and my baby. So I did what I had to do. I filed for unemployment, looked for a job and in the meantime, as an income filler, I was helping entrepreneurs with their bookkeeping and setting up QuickBooks files. I started helping a few people that I knew just here and there to make ends meet. The business owners that I helped were very pleased with my work and started recommending me to their friends and networks.

During this time I continued to go to countless job interviews for months; I could not get a break. Either the jobs that wanted me offered too little pay and wanted an enormous amount of my time or I was "over qualified" for the position. One day I decided just to make myself sound a little more professional when I met with new people to work with; I thought that I should at least come up with a business name. I came up with PG Financial Solutions where the PG stands for Profit and Growth. At that point the start of my entrepreneurial journey began and the rest is history. And you know, I never did find another "dream career or job", instead I created one.

Being an entrepreneur is hard work and don't ever let anyone tell you any different. It is like walking into a dark unrecognizable room where you have to maneuver around blindfolded until you become familiar with the dangers and the comforts of the unknown room. It is not until you have mastered the unknown blindly that you get to remove your blindfold of feelings of fulfillment. I know you are thinking: if that is what entrepreneurship feels like then why on earth would anyone subject themselves to that on purpose. It is the going after a vision that no one else sees with the assurance that even if it fails, it was worth fighting to see. It is at that junction that one can separate an entrepreneur from a typical worker.

I decided to continue with my vision and dream to own my own business because come to find out, I was actually good at what I was doing! In addition I liked to see my clients get results and finally be able to have someone explain to them what their numbers were actually saying. They appreciated someone providing explanations instead of just being given a document and left to interpret it on their own. I actually found out who I really was while building my business. I tapped into my inner strength to have a vision and work that vision into reality. Being an entrepreneur for me is all about continuing to dream and the ability to continue to grow, develop and learn from my mistakes. I realized that I had the courage to take risks that sometimes seem too risky to someone that doesn't understand the vision. I also found out that I had enough endurance to not quit even when I had every reason to. The thought and realization of "ME" being an entrepreneur was so far off my radar, that it wasn't until I actually found myself through my entrepreneur journey that I decided that this "ship" was indeed for me.

Being an entrepreneur has its own set of rewards and obstacles. Adding to that being a mother and wife just deepens the magnitude of some of those rewards and obstacles. Often times, I remind myself of the words to a popular gospel song "I just can't give up now; I come too far from where I started from. Nobody told me, the road would be easy; but I don't believe he brought me this far to leave me..." There were times I really wanted to just give up my dream of having a successful business and just go look for a job and again I can say I'm glad I held on. I have had my company since 2010 and through the years there have been many changes (both good and bad), as well as many blessings and lessons learned.

When I started, I had no idea what it took to own a business. Although I had an accounting degree and had also obtained a master's in business, learning to run a business was not something I was taught. Like many people that enter entrepreneurship, all I knew how to do was do the work. I had no idea the magnitude of what I was getting into. I didn't know how to get new clients outside of word of mouth. Although I was able to sustain my business for years without doing any real marketing, had I understood the importance of doing so a lot of my low points in business may have not been so low. For example, when I started out I had clients that were on contract for monthly work. Had I known in the beginning that I should always look for new clients even when things are comfortable, I would not have been hit so hard in the event that a client, for whatever reason, decided they no longer wanted to work together. That type of financial change brings about issues both professionally and personally. As the business owner, losing even one client was a blow to my ego and caused me to temporarily lose confidence in my business. It is an even bigger blow if the client's payment is a significant part of your income.

When even a portion of your income is lost everything like bills and services offered are affected. Being a single mom, (I was a single mom for the majority of my entrepreneurial journey) I had no time for uncertainty in income. The loss of income was especially devastating for me when I didn't have the amount of clients to pick up the slack, but my bills didn't care, my son's needs didn't care, and life just didn't care. I had to take those skills and go get it regardless of the impact of the blow. It took me having this happen a few times before I figured that I had to ensure that I had clients continually coming in. Because of that, I read everything I could about branding and marketing I even got a business coach to help me create a system to continually get new clients to ensure that my family and my business wouldn't be hit so hard if a client ever decides to leave again.

When I really decided to focus on building a sustainable business I had to let go of a lot of things and people. My focus was on getting my business to really bloom and ensure I was able to provide for my son. Separation, loneliness and depression are real y'all. There were days where I felt alone because I didn't have anyone that understood why I wanted to keep building my business when I could be making a whole lot more money just working a job. It was hurtful at times mainly because I didn't have anyone that could offer any solutions to my issues, insecurities and fears. Of course my mom and family were there to help me if I needed it, but actually understanding and offering more than a nodding head just wasn't there.

It was during this time that I strengthened my faith and relationship with God. I was able to talk to God about my problems. I was doing a lot of work, but I knew that God was my source, not my clients nor my works. I knew that it was God that put that vision and dream within me and that I couldn't give up no matter how alone I felt, how depressed I got or how misunderstood

I became. He sustained me for my son and family as well as for my business.

Over the years, in an effort to becoming a better business owner, I had to make a lot of sacrifices that sometimes affected my son a little more than it should. Sacrifices like bringing work home and working while I could have been spending time with my son. Imagine getting up early to take your child to school and then going into the office to work, working all day and when you get home, you are STILL working. This is not a healthy cycle for anyone especially not a mom of a young child that needs your time and attention. Some nights when I had to bring work home, I would put it on pause to spend a few uninterrupted hours with my son and then once he was sleeping I would get back to work. This was not healthy because I was not getting much sleep; but you do what you have to do when you have to do it.

I have also been in a position where I had to make a decision to not pay some personal bills in order to pay some business bills. This didn't happen often, but at one point when my business was low on income I had to decide if I was going to pay for day care or the subscriptions to my accounting software. I paid the subscriptions and kept my son out of day care for a week. During that week my son stayed in the office with me. It was distracting but I knew if I kept my subscriptions I was able to keep working and able to make more money. The one occasion that this happened caused me to feel like a failure of a mom and business owner. I started to think maybe I should go get a "job" because if I had to make those kinds of decisions then maybe this entrepreneurship thing was not for me.

Even through all the obstacles thrown my way that caused me to doubt myself in business and as a mother, I was still able to maintain a debt free business and help hundreds of clients all while being a pretty awesome mom. As a matter of fact I believe that being an entrepreneur has made me a better mother and also a better wife. See in the beginning of my journey I had just gotten out of a serious relationship with my then fiancé and son's father. Ending that relationship caused so much anxiety and stress in my life because I couldn't really handle the fact that the person that I loved and thought I was going to marry was no longer a part of my life in that capacity. I felt resentment, anger, and jealousy towards him and our situation because I felt like I was left to fight this world alone with a brand new baby when that was not how I had planned my life. It especially was not how I planned to bring a child into this world.

I finally learned to maneuver in the business world as a solopreneur and a single mother of one. Business was good, I was on a steady upward beat, I was growing spiritually, my bank account was growing and I was able to spend time with my son, my friends and family. However around year four I felt the desire to be in a relationship again. I had this desire coupled along with the demands of giving my business a facelift through new services and streamlined processes. I prayed for everything that I desired and I also asked that God prepare me to receive what he had for me personally and professionally. That year I met my now husband Chris. He is totally different from anyone I have ever dated before. Our relationship got serious pretty fast; as a matter of fact I knew he was the one very early in our relationship. He understands me in a way that no one ever has. I also liked the fact that he didn't let me just say any and everything. He has always had a way of checking me in a respectful way.

When we were dating we both brought a son into the picture from a previous serious relationship. Fortunately we were able to successfully blend our families. He says he asked me to marry him because he liked my hustle and the fact that I get things done no matter what. He also saw me as a good mother to my son and a good mother figure to his as well. He called it "wife-able characteristics". I called it just doing what I was supposed to be doing. We dated for a little over a year and got engaged and married within the second year of our relationship. Once we got married I went from one son to three, from single to engaged to married, and from doing well in business to being able to increase my business income almost four times over the course of a year.

After getting married and having four other people that I had to consider along with my business, life got interesting to say the least. The foundations I built early in my entrepreneurial journey really prepared me to be a better mother and wife. It helped because my business taught me how to prioritize, how to utilize my flexibility and how to enjoy the fruits of my labor. "If everything is important, then nothing really is". This statement really hits home with me in regards to my business and my family. By being an entrepreneur, I have the responsibility of all functions of a business as well as taking care of my clients. So prioritizing is incredibly vital.

I have used this skill in dealing with my family as well. I learned to figure out which things need to be done and then I decide which are the most important. By ranking tasks that come up or tasks that are expected, I can choose wisely what to spend my time on and what can really wait. This has been an awesome tool to implement with raising children because time is our most valuable asset. In our personal and our professional lives, if we all continue to treat everything as an important task and fail to prioritize, nothing would get done and as a result everyone would suffer. I am able to choose which events to attend, which activities my kids are involved in and things that we do individually or as a family. The biggest thing I learned from prioritizing is that everything doesn't deserve my attention and what has my attention, deserves my full attention.

Flexibility is probably one of the best things about being an entrepreneur in regards to raising children and having a family. When I was growing up my mom attended every field trip I had, every parent meeting at my school, every performance I had (I was involved in everything imaginable from dance, to karate, to sports, girl scouts, band, you name it). My mom was then and is still now my biggest fan, I mean that lady was there for everything! Just the fact that I knew she was going to be there to support me no matter what, gave me the confidence to try anything and give it my all. I remember growing up seeing other kids hurt because their parents weren't able to come on field trips or to their performances. I vowed that if I were to have kids I wanted to be all about my kids. I wanted to support them in everything that they did and be their biggest cheerleader. I can say being in control of my time has allowed me to be there for my kids. I am able to be their classroom mom, go on all their field trips, go to all their games and practices, take them to birthday parties, even get them at a drop of a dime if an emergency happens at school. This is probably one of the biggest reasons that I fought so hard to grow and keep my business. Seeing the smiles on my kids' faces when I show up for them makes it all worth it.

An even bigger benefit is the fact that I now get to stay home with my third son who is approaching one year old. This is an awesome opportunity for me; the bonding that we experience is irreplaceable. Sticking it out and remaining an entrepreneur has afforded me this luxury to be an at home mom and still be able to make a significant income. Had I not been an entrepreneur, I do believe that as a mother my time with them would be greatly affected in ways that I am not willing to take a gamble.

The last major way being an entrepreneur has made me a better mother is it has allowed me to enjoy the fruits of my labor. I have the money to take my children on multiple trips a year, which is very important to me. I feel that children only dream as far as they are exposed and I feel it is my duty as a mom to expose them to different cultures, foods, places, activities and experiences. One thing I know for sure, a child may not remember all the things we sacrifice to buy them; however they tend to remember experiences you share with them. And being an entrepreneur has allowed me to make it happen with the time flexibility, the money, and the ability to work from any location I choose

I know that I have hit hard on the obstacles, the hardships, and some of the unpopular things I have experienced in entrepreneurship, but that is only because it's unfair to only show case the high points of being your own boss without the balance of the often untold truths of the downsides. One thing that people fail mention when they talk about being an entrepreneur, a mom and a wife is the many hats you wear in a day. They don't tell you that when you are at work, working your business you are in a dominate role where you take charge, give out orders and tend to have to be the lead on everything. Then with your children you have to be a nurturer, a peacemaker, a disciplinarian and more domesticated. Further, if you are married you add on being submissive to your husband, supporting, listening and engaging. All these different roles we as women take on most of the time all in one day. I have learned to stay encouraged and to stay strong because I was built for this and so are you.

Even through the many losses my gains have always replaced and exceeded what I lost. In spite of the fears I overcame every obstacle stronger than when I started. Going through separation, depression, doubt, and loneliness I came out with my faith stretched, tried and assured. As a matter of fact not only has entrepreneurship made me a better mother and wife; it has made me a more patient person, a stronger person, a more compassionate person and an all-around better person. I wouldn't change anything that I've gone through and experienced on my entrepreneurial journey because it all made it a journey worth traveling and I look forward to it's many turns, twists and rewards to come. I am living my dreams on my terms and that is the biggest reason why it all was and still is worth it.

ABOUT THE AUTHOR

Born in Jackson, Mississippi, Tanya Sanders-Kelker is a wife, mother of three boys, sister, daughter, friend, as well as an accomplished accounting professional and business owner. Tanya is a self-proclaimed foodie that enjoys traveling with her family and has a pallet for eclectic music. She is a two-time graduate of Jackson State University with a BBA in Accounting and MBA in operations management. She has dedicated her career to excel in the areas of financial literacy and developing business strategies for increased profits and business growth for business owners. Tanya's unique approach has earned her recognition as "The Entrepreneur's Accountant" and includes a diverse portfolio of work at Profit and Growth, LLC, which she began in 2010.

Having recognized that many businesses need not only someone to do their accounting, but a business partner to help coach them through the numbers of their business; Tanya discovered the opportunity to provide solutions to a plethora of entrepreneurs specifically in the beauty and service industries.

In an effort to further evolve the outlook of accounting to entrepreneurs, Tanya offers personal and business financial coaching programs, virtual services to accommodate clients around the globe, as well as offering in demand products for businesses to help excel them to new levels in business. Her deep passion and commitment to the advancement of small businesses, will assure that Profit and Growth, LLC remains the ultimate resource for businesses in the beauty and service industries.

To learn more about Tanya Sanders-Kelker, MBA visit:

www.tanyaskelker.com
Email: info@pgfinancialsolutions.com
Instagram: @thebeautyaccountant
Facebook: www.facebook.com/thebeautyaccountant

Chapter Nine

Managing Partnerships, Parenthood & Presentations
By: Colette Glover-Hannah

The Motivation

I signed up for this. I chose to have three children and to start my own company.

To all the mothers of children who do their very best every single day to mentally, physically and emotionally pour all they have into their children. To the ones who are writing this 'Journey through Motherhood' manual as we work and walk through life, taking a page from the playbook of our mothers and grandmothers, this country's self-proclaimed Mother-in-Chief, the mothers of ministries, the dentist and her assistant, the fictional Claire Huxtable or the mom who owns the hair salon. For those who trade parenting advice like recipes and those who find themselves repeatedly flirting with their desire to take a leap of faith and abandon their jobs to start their own businesses. This is also for those who often wonder out loud about the 'what ifs' in life.

Recognizing and honoring the spirits of my introduction to womanhood, my great, great-grandmother Martha Wilson, great-grandmother Rosa Elois Henderson, my Grandmother Lizzie Mae Stevenson and my mother Margaret Claritt. I have questioned if entrepreneurship is learned or in my DNA. I am convinced that it is the latter. During a period when women, especially Black women in the South had to follow their husband's lead toward a hint of economic success, I am so proud of the pioneering mothers of my ancestry who moved forward and made a comfortable life for their families and a better one for the next generation. I stand tall because they held their heads high and withstood the ills of a society that constantly told them they were less than because of their gender and race and that they could not and should not attempt to excel. This is why every time I felt, and continue to feel defeated or insecure in my entrepreneurship or parenting endeavors, I pull on their strength and the examples they set for me. My wish to be a part of their successful mother's mantel is what pushes and inspires me so that generations to come will also speak of me in the same breath. My desired legacy is for my children and children's children for many generations to come to honor my unwavering commitment as a mother and resolute courage as a business owner. My journey as a mompreneur can be summarized that simply.

The History

Entrepreneurship was not a new concept to me. I just did not realize that I was familiar with it until I started to build my company Hannah's Shoebox, an online retail shoe store that provides self-esteem and confidence to girls who wear women sizes. Through the website we sell age-appropriate shoes to girls in women sizes providing the styles they want in the sizes they need. Last year another layer was added to the business that includes selling shoes to non-profits and agencies that provide shoes for their clients.

I was introduced to entrepreneurship as a little girl when I was blessed to see my great-grandmother, also known as Mama Dotsey, run her business. She had watched her mother, Martha Wilson, run multiple businesses in the early part of the century. During the 1970s Mama Dotsey owned a very small bar on a dirt road next to the railroad tracks in a rural Florida town called Parrish. We lived in the house next door that she also owned so I was able to closely observe her (when it was closed to the public) run this juke joint as a sole proprietor. I still remember the way she managed the beer and liquor inventory every week. She coordinated with vendors and made sure the soda machine and chip racks were stocked with her customers' favorite flavors and that the jukebox always had the latest and most popular R&B singles in rotation. Watching her write numbers in her weekly ledger probably gave me my first sense of accounting and that women ran and managed businesses. She was certainly my first female entrepreneur role model.

The Reason

Look, I will give you the end of this story in the beginning. Building a business is a frightening experience. There you have it. Let's just get that out at the very beginning. For years I have answered the question about what it's like to leave a 'good' job and start a business or respond to the statement from those who say, "I wish I could do what you did."

For additional insight, look at what the entrepreneurial women around us are doing. According to the 2016 State of Women-Owned Business Report from American Express OPEN:

- Women are starting 1,072 new businesses per day;
- Women-owned businesses generate 1.6 trillion in revenues;
- The number of women-own firms has grown at five times the national average (45% versus 9%);
- Since 2007, 79% of new businesses have been started by women of color.

I have come to embrace my role as a mompreneur, a female business owner who actively balances the role of a mother and being an entrepreneur. To start a business while parenting is double the anxiety because of all the obvious reasons. Someone is depending on you while you must navigate the maze of the countless documents required to legally begin and maintain a company. In addition you must be a mother to those who depend on you each day for basic things such as food, shelter, clothing and emotional support. At some point you really don't know where the business requirements begin and the parental duties for that day end. Sometimes you will merge the two responsibilities and pray that they do not interfere with or cancel out the intended outcomes of each side. It is confusing and comforting at times and other times a bit chaotic. You will find that on any given day there is no script or calendar that will help you figure things out. In some occurrences you can only depend on your body's organs to get you through and even they are in an occasional conflict. The head, heart and gut are the compass for direction on many days when those things that 'pop up' arise – and they certainly will do just that, pop up.

The Story:

My ability to display my entrepreneurship acumen was revealed while an Associate Vice President at the University of South Florida. There I built the institution's first Community Relations Department from scratch in the early 2000s, during a time when very few universities or companies were concerned about community outreach. In addition to the department, I created and oversaw the implementation of several sustainable programs that raised the brand and visibility of the institution. This talent of creating operations turned out to be my trial run toward building things that people wanted and needed. Recently I delivered a keynote address at USF and highlighted several of the programs that were built during my tenure. Some instances were included to show how every single person in the audience could also work to build their own institutional legacy, while the other was to introduce the entrepreneurial leadership that we all should have to expand the reach of services we provide in our careers.

After working in higher education for 15 years, I decided to leave the university and begin my career as a Community Relations Consultant. This was my first brush with life as a mompreneur. The initial challenge I had with this new venture was time management. I learned early on to work smarter, not longer. I needed to manage my calendar so I could meet the obligations of my clients while making sure I met the needs of my children. My calendar consisted of taking my children to school in the mornings, heading to the gym for a quick workout and then back home before heading out to meetings from 10 a.m. to 2 p.m. When possible, I would not schedule meetings after 2 p.m. because I needed to pick my children up from school before 3:15. We would come home and I would put on my mommy hat to do the chores and assignments of being an engaged parent. I admit that there were some days when I quickly prepared or picked up dinner and rushed through homework or evening conversations with the kids because I was thinking about putting the finishing touches on a report or creating an agenda for the next day's meeting.

The hardest part of the day would occur after 10 p.m. when I would begin saying goodnight to the kids and then go to the other room to work on the computer until around midnight or 1 a.m. often falling asleep at the terminal. I am certainly not complaining about these options that I adopted for myself, but I quickly learned that there had to be a more efficient way of managing my time. Those who know me understand that I am a person who needs a significant amount of sleep to function and be cordial during the day. This manner of operation was not good for me nor anyone around me-due to inefficiencies of managing my day. Realizing this, I changed things around so I would only meet with people on certain days of the week. When given the option I would have at least two working days when I blocked myself off as unavailable on my calendar so that I could get assignments done for my business. Another lesson I learned very early was that being a mompreneur can be very lonely, especially if you once worked in a large environment that had water cooler conversations, mini-lunch gatherings and birthday celebrations in the break room.

After noticing that I had slipped into this space, I then decided to offer my clients a few hours a week of onsite time. This was a win-win for both of us. They could have face-to-face time with me and I had a chance to be around adults and engage in adult conversation. Before this discovery, the only interesting dialogue I had was with the people in my home. Though I enjoyed our dinner conversations, these were very different exchanges from the ones I needed to have to keep my finger on the pulse of my profession.

The Start of the Entrepreneurial Journey

After a few years as a Community Relations Consultant, I one day got an idea for a new business. I am convinced that most start-ups begin this way. I often think about the ideas that come along and we talk ourselves out of their creation. Every time someone says "there should be a this" or "I wish someone would invent that" or, of course, the things that are missing in your life and you know that you are not the only one suffering without it. Yes, that thing.

When my daughter started school I will admit that I was so happy for one single requirement – that was school uniforms. I never had to think about 'school clothes.' She started her academic career at a Montessori school that required red or blue shirts with their logo and parents could choose to purchase khaki or navy blue shorts, skirts or dresses. Life was so simple for a then 3-year-old to get up and get ready for school. With her daily chosen uniform attire, she would add Mary Jane shoes to her Monday-Thursday ensemble and her sneakers on Friday. Sounds simple and convenient to most parents. This was until my daughter was five years old and in a size 5 shoe. She was on the verge of crossing over into the adult women sizes and I was about to panic because finding Mary Janes in adult women sizes was extremely difficult. Then my daughter's age began to match her shoe size. The next year at age six she was in a size six and so on and so on. Fast-forward to the fifth grade and my daughter was 11 years old and in a size 11 shoe. I had grown more frustrated at not being able to find her shoe size in most stores and more importantly, not finding something that was age-appropriate for a little girl who happened to have larger feet.

That year the Christmas season came and I was so excited to have found a beautiful, festive holiday dress for an annual Holiday dinner celebration that we attend. The dress was perfect; I then set out to find the matching shoes. I went to every department store at every mall in our county and then neighboring counties. I ventured out to other parts of the state as well as searched online for the simplest style of shoe in a women's size 11. I was so upset. I simply wanted a cute pair of age-appropriate black shoes to match my daughter's red, black and white holiday dress. I gave in and purchased a pair of plain black flats and felt so disappointed. After sharing my failed shopping quest with family members, someone suggested I open a store to address the issue that we knew so many parents of tween girls also faced.

I would not be telling the truth if I pretend that I was not nervous and afraid to start Hannah's Shoebox. The doubt associated with taking a dream from concept to revenue, in most cases is consuming, overwhelming and very demanding. There was a distinct sense of being afraid that this may not work, combined with the feeling that this was going to be the best business ever.

There were plenty of nights of sitting at my computer trying to literally talk myself through those initials hurdles. "I am smart. I can do this. I will not be defeated by this," are a few affirmations that I recited to myself repeatedly. In the same deep breath that I took in frustration while choosing a website template, I would also exhale in excitement because it was a step toward building my unique business. I learned early that I had to celebrate the little accomplishments because each one was critical to the overall success of this company.

The Mom:

As a mother there are periods in our lives when parenting consists of a set daily, weekly, monthly, and then annual scheduling. Years ago, when I pulled out of the office parking lot, I left work behind until the next day. If you are mompreneur you learn to throw all the scheduling out the window. There will be no predicted routines and you never figuratively pull away from the parking lot. I noticed a huge difference in my home/life schedule when I was employed by the university versus my life today. I share the thought with many others that a work/life balance does not exist and that I am learning that doing my best is simply all that I can offer—I have accepted it. In the early stages of a start-up business you are always, always working. You don't get to turn it off or go home. You trade five, eight-hour days for much longer hours that begin to just run on into one another. Running your business in its early stages is a 24/7 commitment. Little things become big things. I share with others this transition into a mompreneur was truly real for me when thoughts and ideas for my business would awaken me in the middle of the night. The thought takes on a very loud voice and it literally wakes you up. You realize that the 'just one more thing' is a lie that you occasionally tell yourself as you feel the need for an excuse to restart the computer or compose another email message.

One day I was talking with my daughter's fourth grade teacher, Ms. Rostick during a parent-teacher conference. Ms Rostick shared with me that my daughter was excelling in her class and she wanted to give her more challenging assignments. I looked in her eyes as she was speaking to me, but I swear I was not really listening. I had a child who was graduating from college that year and another was a senior in high school and about to enter college. I remember thinking about the needs of both seniors while she was talking about my daughter's assignments. I was also having slight anxiety about a major event coming up for my school district client. Had all the details been addressed, the technology needs email sent, do I have the cell phone numbers of all tomorrow's speakers. All this while looking her dead in her eyes and nodding my head in agreement with everything she suggested. I thanked Ms. Rostick for her observation of my daughter's skills and summed up my life at that moment. "Ms. Rostick, I parent in rotation. I have a son about to graduate from college and one who's entering. It is not Elois' turn right now. So, whatever you think you need to do to better prepare her for next year, please do it. I trust you as her teacher."

Meanwhile, during all of this there are times when you struggle and question your role as a parent. There is still a debate around the possibility of maintaining a work-life balance. Many working parents really believe that we can have it all and strive for the notion that balance is always 50/50. As a parent of three children, I subscribe to the belief that balance does not exist.

For example, I have been blessed to attend nearly every event my daughter has ever participated in from PreK-3 to sophomore year of high school. Recently, she had a choral performance at school (no solo or individual role) and I needed to attend an event for networking purposes with someone who was in the country for the evening. Although I knew my husband and mother would be in the audience to cheer loudly after each selection, I intensely struggled with my absence from her performance for some time. This incident is an illustration of how mompreneurs or working moms, struggle to make decisions between being present for our children or to attend another event that takes us away from them. There are also the tradeshows and conferences that take us away from our darling sons and daughters for extended periods. The ability to effectively run multiple offices and customers in neighboring counties or around the country takes master scheduling techniques and skills.

This parental pull can be potentially devastating to a business. Last summer my daughter was selected to participate in a Leadership Program for Girls at Princeton University. The event took place the first week in August, which was great because my calendar was clear. We were both excited and spent all summer anticipating the trip. That was until a new customer, a private school that cleared the way for me to sell uniform shoes to its parents, moved their Open House back a couple of weeks to the exact time that I would be at Princeton with my daughter. I could not believe that this was actually happening. Lord knows, I could not afford to abandon this new deal with the school and I would never not go with my daughter to introduce her to the possibilities of Princeton. After much thought and prayer, I called a friend and asked her to stand in for me at the Open House to sell the shoes. After giving her a crash course on Hannah's Shoebox offerings and prices, she agreed. My son offered to assist her and the two of them were able to manage the uniform shoe sales. They did well, however, the trade-off was that they fell short of the projected sells for the day. I quickly concluded that any money was better than no money and I was extremely grateful that they had saved the day and that account.

The Assistance

Please do not think that I one day said that I would start a business and it magically appeared. Lord knows it was not that easy by a long shot. I discussed the Hannah Shoebox concept with my husband and laid out the plans to begin implementing the idea. I spent many, many, many hours at the local Small Business Development Center talking with their counselors and accessing the invaluable resources they had available that would have cost me literally thousands of dollars to purchase. I also took full advantage of my membership with the Centre for Women in Business, participated in 1MillionCups and worked closely with the local Entrepreneurship Collaborative Center's business counselors. All of this was available to me for free or very little cost. I will always be grateful for these services and encourage other business owners to utilize their expertise. I spoke with other moms and family members about my concept. I knew that I had a decent idea when others would give me the same look after explaining the business. Their eyes would get big and they would say, "I needed this when I was little," or "this is exactly what I need for my daughter(s)." This informal market research was exactly what I needed to ensure that my concept was worth bringing to market and that it would generate revenue.

The Challenges

Funny how life interrupts our plans sometimes. Just when you have figured out your next move it simply forces you to regroup. During the early period of becoming a mompreneur, my husband worked in sales for a major network company. He was outstanding at his job as he consistently ranked in the top 10 in the nation's top sales representatives for the corporation. About one year after launching Hannah's Shoebox with a website, inventory and other items purchased with the initial thousands of dollars we had invested into the company, my husband became ill with an undiagnosed condition that literally knocked him off his feet. His condition left him unable to work full time, then as the condition worsened he was unable to work at all. His job loss during this period became the least of our worries. We learned the reason his body was failing him. He had CANCER and it was aggressive. We were then faced with the largest obstacle that I had to overcome in my life and certainly since starting this business. The business quickly became an afterthought to making sure my husband's life was sparred, that he received the best local care we could find and that his cancer would be conquered. Let me share with you that absolutely nothing was done for my company during this period. Phone calls from distributors were intentionally sent to voicemail and not one shoe promotion ran during this period. I was a company of one and all of my attention was directed toward my husband's health. The days were filled with internet cancer research and appointments and conversations with doctors for second, third, fourth, fifth, sixth and seventh opinions for care options. I called every friend I knew in the cancer-related healthcare industry and ran his diagnosis by them to get their insight and opinions. Eventually, my husband had surgery to remove the cancer and then immediately faced complications from the operation that required additional hospitalizations and added procedures. The longtime recuperation was a physical and emotional toll on our entire family. This was by far the most horrific time in our lives.

The Return

After we returned to a rhythm in our breathing and gained a sense that my husband was on his way to recovery, I could get back to Hannah's Shoebox. The first order of business was to decide if I would continue to pursue my passion and build this unique online shoe store or go get a regular, steady, reliable job with guaranteed income. I was so torn, because when I started this mompreneur journey we were in a very good financial place that offered great health insurance, a benefits package, lots of perks and allowed us to live a very comfortable lifestyle on one salary. I now had to make a decision that impacted my entire family. The weight of this choice was like none that I had ever felt in my entire life.

One thing that helped to tilt my decision was the financial discipline we had shown under my husband's guidance and our engaged financial advisor. I prayed constantly and then decided to continue to pursue my vision for Hannah's Shoebox. I was so invested financially and physically into this company that I could not abandon my dream and that I would continue with even more determination to build this business. It hasn't been easy for me nor my family to build this company, but I am still proud and happy with the outcomes. There were a few days when I questioned my decision to move forward, and I admit that doubt still rears its ugly head occasionally, but it is far outnumbered by the belief that I am on the right path and fulfilling my purpose and passion.

The Results

Each day I work on my business in some capacity. I have always been able to move forward because I have sacrificed so much. I genuinely love what I'm doing.

I learned through this mompreneur journey that I am stronger, smarter and far more resilient that I knew. While running a very demanding business, I sometimes amaze myself by creating and managing all aspects of this business from concept to implementation while having raised two college educated sons and still parenting a very smart and active daughter. I juggle many responsibilities and sometimes, thanks to the advice of my sister-in-law who is in the medical profession, things are simply addressed in a triage manner. Who or what is "bleeding" the most is the thing that deserves to get my attention at that time. Sometimes it will be my family and other times it will be the business.

The Reflection

In my quiet morning time between meditation and the morning news, I find myself asking about my intentions for doing certain things in my life. The answer that I have the majority of the time comes back to the three humans that I birthed. They are the reason I do so many things and work so darn hard as a mompreneur when it would be so much easier to work differently and a more predictable life. For me easy has never been easy. I am very conscious of the behaviors I model for my children, especially my daughter. Strength and determination is in my blood, but I know I have been able to persevere in seemingly hard times because I watched my mother struggle. No, she wasn't an entrepreneur, but she managed to earn a college degree after getting married at the age of 18 then separating and later divorcing my father in her mid-20s. I watched my mother work hard to earn the best grades that she needed to maintain the grant that was paying for her college education. I watched her achieve this as a divorced mother of two young girls while living barely above the federal guidelines for poverty. Occasionally she took us with her to the campus library and her classroom when she was unable to secure a babysitter. My sister and I would sit in the corner of her college classroom with M&Ms and watch mom participate in the conversations. This was my model of motherhood and stick-to-itiveness. Mother graduated from college and eventually retired as a school teacher after 36 years. She would not and did not quit regardless of life's circumstances. Therefore, I shall never quit.

The Advice
MOMPRENEUR TIPS

1) *Be Present*. Whether spending time at the office, with a customer or your family, BE where you are and give them your undivided attention.

2) *Use your Village*. Create and utilize the village collection of family and friends to assist with your children and/business needs.

3) *Be Strategic and Efficient*. Schedule your meetings and commitments so that they feed into each other when possible.

4) *Manage your Time*. Learn that NO is a complete sentence and sometimes necessary in the workplace and at home. I have found it to be a very liberating word.

5) *Your Children Can Work*. Small children love to help with tasks like putting stamps on letters and older kids can put tape

on boxes and alphabetize files. Teens are great for managing social media sites and assisting at trade fairs and other events.

6) *Communicate.* Let your family know your situation and circumstances. They can celebrate your victories and support you in your setbacks.

7) *Build a Network.* Join other professionals who are driven toward building successful companies. Create an informal advisory board of accomplished men and women in varied professions who will hold you accountable and help you grow your company.

8) *Utilize Resources.* There are so many local and national resources for women to get information for running a successful business. Also, explore online databases for up-to-date information.

9) *Health is Wealth.* Remember to take care of your health in this mompreneur journey. There is only one of you so make time for your physical, mental, emotional and spiritual fitness.

10) *Remember the Why.* Never ever forget why you developed a passion to pursue this dream. Write it down and look at it every day.

ABOUT THE AUTHOR

R. Colette Glover-Hannah is the Founder and CEO of Hannah's Shoebox, an online shoe store that provides self-esteem and confidence to girls who women size shoes. The ecommerce store, with customers throughout the United States and Canada, has been featured on several network television shows, radio stations, newspapers and magazines publications.

Hannah's Shoebox was born after Colette, a mother, became frustrated with the absence of age-appropriate shoes in the footwear industry available for her then 11-year-old tween daughter. She created and launched the online store with the intentions of becoming the one-stop shop for families who want to purchase cute, stylish shoes for young teens that will allow them to look their age instead of mature adults.

In addition to individual online sales, the store is an exclusive or approved vendor with K-8 public and private schools that have required uniform policies and services non-profit organizations that purchase shoes for Girls' Organizations and/or Programs. Hannah's Shoebox has been recognized by the Centre for Women in Business in the InnovatHER competition, Tampa Bay Minority Enterprise Development Week winner of the PITCH competition and as a 1Million Cups-Tampa participant. The company was selected to participate in the competitive Greater Tampa Chamber of Commerce Startup Scholars program and the Community Incubator of the University of Tampa's John P. Lowth Center for Entrepreneurship. Hannah's Shoebox is a certified woman/minority-owned business with several government agencies.

Colette is married to Chadwick and the mother of two adult sons, Ryan (Howard University alumnus) and Chadwick (University of Cincinnati alumnus) and a teen daughter, Elois. She earned a bachelor's degree from Florida A&M University and her master's from the University of South Florida. She was appointed to the Greater Tampa Chamber of Commerce Board of Directors; Friends of Joshua House Foundation, Inc. Board of Directors; The Centre for Women in Business Advisory Council; Tampa Bay Committee of the Akilah Institute for Women in Kigali, Rwanda and the Executive Board of Black Women Business Owners, Executives and Entrepreneurs. She is a member of Alpha Kappa Alpha Sorority, Inc., Tampa Bay Women in Networking and the Greater Tampa Chamber of Commerce-Women of Influence. Colette is an alumna of Leadership Hillsborough, Leadership Tampa and Leadership Tampa Bay.

www.hannahsshoebox.com
info@hannahsshoebox.com
Facebook: facebook.com/hannahsshoebox
Twitter: @hannahsshoebox
Instagram: @tweenshoes

Chapter Ten

Mommy Means Business
By: Melissa Alexander

Melissa, you did what?

Melissa who?

This will likely be the reaction from most people who know me when they read this. Why? Because I have never uttered a word about writing a book or had the desire to write a book. Well except for that one time when I was going through a period of "men really have no idea what women want" and I thought "maybe I should write a book about that" . However that thought came and left my mind pretty quickly as I am more of a behind the scenes kind of person. As a matter of fact I have been the cheerleader for a few of my friends encouraging them to write a book. I must share the short version of how I came to be a part of this amazing book collaboration before I get into the guts of my mompreneur journey. I hope it inspires someone else to leap!

The first time I saw a social media post about the opportunity for the book collaboration my initial thought was "what will I write about?" and "who's going to read it?" The book was about women who have conquered something in their lives. I've conquered a few things in life but which one would fit? Which one would make an impact?

During the time of my "debate with myself" and before I had the chance to silence my "Negative Nancy" thoughts all of the slots were filled for the book collaboration and just like that there went the opportunity for me to be a part of the book collaboration.

I told my husband what happened and he couldn't believe that I didn't jump on the opportunity. He figured after I told him about it I signed up. Nope, shame on me.

Fast forward to August 23, 2016 another book opportunity had been presented, but this time it was geared toward Moms, I was so excited but doubt fell right in again. "What will I write?" and again "Who's going to read it" ....BUT, I thought this was a great opportunity. The thought of the book stayed on my mind all day. Mid-day on the same day my accountability partner sent me a text (we learned about this opportunity through our online Facebook Group) to ask me if I was going to do the book. Keep in mind she didn't even know my thoughts of wanting to do the first book let alone this book so this question caught me off guard. I told her how I had missed out on the first opportunity because of self-doubt. I thought more about it and knew that being published would be great. After a couple more text I said, "I may just take the leap!" "Let's jump together!" she replied. I did not respond as I became busy with other things throughout the day.

Fast forward to the same day around 7:45pm. I was attending Bible Study at a Church which I hadn't attended prior. I did not know anyone nor had I spoken to anyone in the church. As the Pastor was closing God just began speaking through the Pastor and out came the words, "You will write that book, you will be successful." Uh, what? Wait a minute!! Did I just hear what I think

I heard??? I left that Church full of emotion and walked out without even looking up. I hopped in my car and started praising God and had a good ugly cry on my drive home.

By the time all of this really hit me it was late and I wanted to text my accountability partner and simply say, "I am in". However, it was late and I didn't want to chance waking her up. I told myself I would text her in the morning as well as sign up for the book collaboration. REALLY who puts God's confirmation on hold???? Apparently I was about to but…..

I hopped on Facebook to answer a couple of messages and while I was scrolling I saw a video my friend posted. She had posted a video by Lisa Nichols entitled "How to Avoid Procrastination by Leaping Forward." UMMM what was that? Yes, LEAPING (remember I used the word leap when I replied to the text message earlier in the day to my accountability partner). I reposted this video at 11:16 pm as yet another big confirmation.

At 11:28pm someone commented under the video, "Let's go partner". It was my accountability partner, the person whom I did not text for fear she was asleep. Apparently she was awake and at that moment we decided to LEAP! I ran to my smart phone and signed up for the book collaboration!!!! That led me here to this book to share my mompreneur journey with you. So, here it is:

My name is Melissa Alexander and I am the mother of a beautiful and active toddler girl. I am also a godmother and an aunt to beautiful and smart girls whom I pray will never put limits on themselves. I also pray that when all of these girls get older they will read this book and be encouraged to live their dreams both before and after motherhood.

I am an entrepreneur and I wear various hats. In addition to for profit business ventures, I am also the proud founder of a non-profit organization in which we aid the less fortunate and homeless in Georgia by providing basic necessities such as hygiene items, clothes, blankets and food. Over the last year I've had the privilege of being one of the leaders in a women and teen girl conference tour. Our goal through the conferences has been to empower women and teen girls through girl talk pajama jams and mentoring through motivational and interactive workshops with women.

My entrepreneur journey began in college with jewelry sales. My love of jewelry started when I was a little girl watching my mom get dressed. She had so much jewelry and it was all so beautiful. She doesn't know this (she will know now), but when she would leave to go out I would sit in the sink inside of her bathroom and try on her jewelry. Yes, mom I did that! Once I was old enough to purchase my own it was OVER! Back then, and even today, I have jewelry for just about every occasion.

In my hometown is an area that sells wholesale items. As a frugal college student on a budget, I enjoyed shopping there for bold, bright and bulky jewelry. On several occasions people inquired where I had purchased my jewelry. After being asked this same question countless times, I asked a few inquirers if they'd be interested in purchasing some of the jewelry if I brought back a bulk from my hometown. The response was positive and the journey began.

I sold jewelry for awhile in college and eventually revisited the idea some years after college. By this time there were several "build a jewelry business in a box" kind of businesses for which I did not have an interest. The true entrepreneur spirit inside of me knew that I could go out and make and/or purchase wholesale my own jewelry, create a website, have my own business cards and my own marketing plan. It seemed like a lot of work, but in my opinion it beat having to deal with a middle- man. Entrepreneurs that read this know exactly what I am talking about. I am sure they can also relate to those silent yet loud conversations you have in your head by yourself as an entrepreneur. Needless to say I built the business from the ground up. I had days when I really wanted to quit! Working with wholesalers, buying products then realizing I didn't like the quality, attending as many events as I could to get the business name out there. I mean the list goes on and on BUT I did it and I was so proud of myself for not quitting nor taking the easy way out.

I will never forget the time that I attended an intimate women's networking event and we each had to stand up and say who we were and the name of our business. I had heard of at least two of the women there who were popular bloggers and I felt so intimidated and nervous. Once it was my turn I stood up and just wanted to whisper who I was and my little business name. After I said the name of my business a young lady said, "You're the owner of that company? Wow I follow you on Social Media." I can only imagine the expression I had on my face when she said this. I just remember quickly sitting down and thinking that I was doing something right! I don't say this to brag; I say this to encourage you to never give up. Your hard work will pay off and you never know who is watching.

So aside from having a love for jewelry, why did I choose to start other businesses and continue my life as an entrepreneur? The answer is simple: FREEDOM! I could not see myself in a 9 to 5 job permanently. I am not saying anything is wrong with a traditional 9 to 5 as it allowed me many opportunities after college. However, I just knew that a traditional 9 to 5 job would not be in my future forever.

I realized that in a job your salary was the limit and being an entrepreneur your salary has no limit, only the limits that you place on yourself. I really enjoy traveling and serving the community - things that would be restricted as an employee. Last but not least, I watched my mom bust her hump being a nurse working double shifts and not being able to spend as much time as she would have liked with my siblings and I. My mom missed things in my life growing up; not because she wanted to but because she had to work in order to provide. She made sure we didn't go without. I always knew that when the time came for me to start a family I could not be tied to a job. I didn't know how that would work, but that was definitely my desire and prayer.

Both of my parents were "part-time" entrepreneurs when I was growing up. I am a product of "Side Hustle" entrepreneurs. My dad was a veteran and later worked for the government and his "side business" was as a Real Estate Investor. My mom was a nurse and also a network marketer and real estate investor. As I write this I wonder to myself how their lives would have been if they had chosen to turn those side hustles into full time businesses. I will never know, but it will definitely keep my entrepreneur fire burning.

As a mompreneur you will face obstacles. I have found that for the most part having what used to be "my time" is no longer just for me, it has become my daughter's time. I work around my daughter's time and her needs. I can't just jump up like I used to at a moment's notice to attend an event or be on a webinar without worrying about my daughter's needs. However, I would not trade being a mommy for anything in the world. I will be honest and say I miss being able to jump up at a moment's notice or attend networking events at my leisure. Mommies need that time and your business needs it too. As I work on balance I definitely plan to improve and make room for those things again.

I've had plenty of days, and I still do, where my daughter lies next to me in bed asleep and I am on the computer in the middle of the night. Recently she fell asleep during the day in my bed and I just couldn't bring myself to wake her up and put her in her crib. Instead I put a chair in my bathroom nearby, grabbed a TV table for my computer and worked from the bathroom so I could see her if she popped up from her sleep. I know that sounds funny, but that's the type of things that I do to ensure my daughter is good and still take care of my business.

For me being a mommy and an entrepreneur are both full time jobs and I want to give them both eight plus hours each day; however that's nearly impossible. Do I sometimes try to do that? Yes! Do I have "mommy guilt" when I spend hours and hours on my business? Yes, but all the feelings and emotions are worth it when I am able to witness milestones in my daughter's life and watch her grow up daily right before my eyes.

Right now is a great example. As I write this it's 1:41 am on a Sunday morning. I woke up this morning around 7am. I worked on my business for about three hours straight then I went into mommy mode for pretty much the remainder of the day. I did have moments where I was on the phone performing business tasks, but for the most part it was my daughter's day. I shifted my focus to solely business as soon as she was sound asleep.

Speaking of sleep (well in my case a LACK OF SLEEP) I, like most entrepreneurs, have a mind that never quits. My mind is constantly going. Throw in business tasks, a family and other duties- sleep is definitely something I don't get enough of on a daily basis. I've turned down invites for different business events because I am typically tired. If I can't be 100% and represent my companies and myself well I will not attend. I know situations will not always be 100%, but I strive to get as close to it as I can. I do sometimes feel like I miss opportunities, but I have to remind myself that God is in control and He will not allow me to miss the opportunities that are meant for me.

The flip side of this is there are KEYS to overcoming these obstacles or at least managing them. As a person who was in management and customer service for over 15 years, I learned skills that definitely spilled over to entrepreneurship. Keys that have helped me face obstacles as a mompreneur are first and foremost prayer and meditation, getting and staying organized, using a "to do" list, prioritizing and taking a break!

My prayer and meditation time is so important as it calms me and centers me. I am able to quiet all of the outside noise and thoughts and just have my time with God. The days that I run out of the house without prayer and meditation just don't feel right and a lot of times the day doesn't turn out the way I anticipate. So for me this is the number one key. Fulfilling this key allows everything else to fall into place. I remember when we first brought our daughter home from the hospital and we were trying to figure out feeding schedules for her, eating schedules for us, bath time for her and yes bath time for us! A bath - no time for that so let's be real- a quick shower never felt so good. Moms know exactly what I mean.

One day I woke up around 5am and the house was still; it felt like the world had stopped. God said, "This is your time." I knew instantly what God meant but I was like ...um it's 5am, I need to get my sleep when I can and blah blah blah. Needless to say I began to almost instantly pop up each day thereafter around 5am without my daughter crying and without an alarm clock. That became my prayer and meditation time. Once I began to do this it seemed as though everything started to fall in place. My daughter slept later, my husband and I worked out our schedules and we were all more calm and at peace.

You've heard it before an "organized life is a happy life". I really believe this to be true. I am an organized person. Organization is for sure an important key as an entrepreneur and definitely when you have children and living the momrepeneur life. I tell people if you're not organized, hire someone who is and allow them to help you become organized. Let's face it, if you're not organized to some capacity you are going to end up chasing your tail. How many times have you been working and said "I know that document is somewhere around here I was just looking at it yesterday" or how about "where is my son or daughter's coat? He or she just had it on yesterday." Simple struggles indeed, but imagine if you had a system- something simple like hand written files in a file cabinet or box that you could reference when you needed it or could slide that document in once you were done utilizing it or if you had a specific place where you put your children's coats, boots or whatever you choose? I think you get my point. Looking for documents, keys and your children's belongings can be so frustrating and such a waste of time. Think about ways you can organize your business and your mommy life.

Utilizing a "to do list" and prioritizing go hand in hand. Here's the thing: a list is just a bunch of words on a paper if you don't keep the list current and if you are not referencing the list as you complete items on the list. I feel such joy when I check off items from my list. Don't laugh it's true. Surely I am not the only one? I love the sense of accomplishment.

In corporate America as a manager, each day I had a "to do" list an arm's length long and my goal was to address if not complete each one daily. I am this way today with my businesses and in my life as a mom. Writing down what needs to be done in the order of importance is a big help. I am a visual person so for me this works great. I do make notes on my phone and I use the calendar and Google appointments, but for me it always comes back to paper. Find a way to list out your task and prioritize them and you will see the difference.

Yeah, so I am certain that when you read "take a break" you probably rolled your eyes or said "yeah right, when?" I get it! Do I take as many breaks as I should? No, but when my body starts telling me to stop I stop. My goal is to take that break before my body starts telling me to because sometimes when your body starts talking to you it's too late and sickness can set in. Been there done that! Learn from my mistakes and TAKE THAT BREAK! I don't necessarily mean take a week vacation to Mexico. It could be as simple as a "daycation" alone to the mountains or to the beach or to the spa. Hop in the car and go for a drive. Check into a hotel and stay for the day and return home when your children have gone to sleep. Whatever you decide, just a take a break to give your mind and body a rest. You are no good to your kids if you're drained.

Being an entrepreneur has made me a better mother in several areas. Flexibility, patience, multitasking and being organized are a few of the traits that come to mind. As an entrepreneur you quickly learn that you must be flexible; no two days are the same and the same holds true in motherhood.

In business patience is essential and it has also helped me be a better mother. You can't rush feeding time, potty time and overall time with your children. I can think of times when my daughter has been excited about eating a certain food so that's what I had as part of my meal plan for the week. Then out of nowhere she's looking at the food like "what is this? I've never seen or tasted that before in my life". Or times when she's cranky not because she was wet or sleepy, but just because. She has bad days and I can't get mad for she is just a child. Times like these are when you must be flexible and prepare a different meal and patience to prepare that meal and not be upset about doing so.

Women, in my opinion, are the ultimate multi- taskers and organizers. These characteristics have helped me so much as a mother! Just because you have a meeting or a conference call or whatever duty your business calls you to perform, that does not stop a baby from being sick or from a babysitter calling to say that they can't make it. Being able to multitask and being organized will save your sanity.

The year my daughter was born my mother became very sick. The day before my daughter was discharged from the hospital my mother was admitted into the hospital. She was so ill that she was hospitalized for 121 days. I can't begin to put into words how trying of a time that was not only on myself, but also on my siblings. Mentally I was an emotional mess- I was worried about my mom and I was also a new mother. Some days I didn't know if I was coming or going. I had moments when I would leave my mom's side and literally cry out to God in the bathroom because it was hard to watch my mom in that condition. Being the second to the eldest child I felt I had to put on a brave face and that's what I did most days.

I bring this up to say first and foremost prayer comforted me. As I said it's my first key. I really thank God for carrying me. I didn't make it through on my own strength. Second, I have always been pretty well organized with my businesses so when this happened I didn't take as big of a hit as I could have had I not been organized. I was able to spend many hours each day with my mom in the hospital as well as spend time with my newborn daughter. Was everything in place and running smoothly? No not everything, but for the most part it was. Did I spend nights in the hospital on my laptop as my mom slept? Yes, but that was to check and double check systems I had in place. I am happy to say my mom is doing great today and to look at her you would never know what she's been through. I thank God for the work he did in my mom; my mom is a walking testimony. Tough times will come you just have to be ready. STAY READY!

People have asked me on different occasions if it's hard being an entrepreneur. They ask if it is really worth it. My answer is always YES! It's so worth it. Are there hard days? YES! I have had days in which I have told my husband I was going to quit or days when I felt like crying because I was overwhelmed. The fact is there are hard days in a 9-5 as well. There are moments when as an employee people want to cry and they want to quit. However, they keep going. So why wouldn't I keep going for my own business? For me the biggest reason it's all worth it is FREEDOM!

Freedom: freedom to take my daughter to the museum in the middle of the week; freedom to go on vacation without putting in a request for time off and hoping that it will be approved; freedom from not having a cap on how many vacation days I have for the year; freedom to care for my mom once she was discharged from the hospital into my care. I can't imagine not being able to do that for her and I thank God that I had the ability to do so.

Being a mompreneur allows me real life face time with my daughter. She gets all of my attention and lots of quality time. I feel like children really need that face time with their parents. We as parents can miss so much in our children's day to day if we don't have that face time with them. Not only that, but time passes so quickly. My daughter is only a toddler yet I feel like time is passing me by so fast!

I remember the first time she "went" on the potty. I was so ecstatic and overjoyed. I even took a picture. YES, I took a picture. Had I not been home with her I would have missed that. I was there when she took her first step. I didn't have to hear about it or watch it on a video.

As I said previously, it's hard work but it's hard work that I am doing for my family and for myself. I get to build a life that I don't need a vacation from, but a life where I can take a vacation from when I want. Physically I am healthier and mentally I am healthier; these are all a plus in my opinion!

Always remember ASK for what you want, BELIEVE it will happen, RECEIVE, be thankful and Repeat!

ABOUT THE AUTHOR

Born in Texas and currently residing in Georgia, Melissa Alexander is an accomplished CEO of three businesses. Melissa discovered her passion through helping others, which has served as the catalyst in starting her three endeavors, *"Giving Hope 365," "Accessory Chick," and "Social Media Chick."* Through Melissa's desire to serve others and having recognized the large number of individuals living in poverty within the United States, *Giving Hope 365* was founded. The organization provides food and clothes for the homeless as well as assist the underprivileged with basic needs in the state of Georgia. In addition to serving the homeless, Melissa also enjoys empowering women through fashion with her business *Accessory Chick,* which provides unique and affordable jewelry pieces that may be purchased locally in Lawrenceville, GA or online. *Accessory Chick* also offers Home Parties and is available for vendor events.

Social Media Chick was established from Melissa's love of social media engagement, to promote businesses and events for individuals and business owners. Melissa also serves as a leader for *Lovin The Skin I'm In* women and teen girl tour. The goal of this effort is to empower women of all ages through girl talk, mentoring and interactive workshops. Melissa has recently completed her first book collaboration and is looking to expand *Giving Hope 365* to assist more individuals and provide jobs.

To learn more Melissa Alexander visit:
www.acessorychick.net.or www.socialmediachick.net
facebook: Giving Hope 365
facebook: The Accessory Chick
twitter: Accesorychick1
instagram: Acessorychick1
facebook: The Social Media Chick
twitter: Socialmediachick
instagram: Socialmediachick
phone: 678.619.1033

Chapter Eleven

Turning Dreams Into Reality
By: Jennifer Logan

I have worked in retail management all of my career, I have specialized in human resources for the past 20 years. I have a true passion for all aspects of human resources and have accelerated my career in becoming an HR Guru. The most intriguing aspect of human resources that I have grown most fond of is training and development. I have gained a lot of education and experience in developing content and facilitating. In my years of hands on experience I have gained knowledge on running a billion-dollar business. Meshing my education, certifications and years of actual practice in my specialized field of human resources, I decided to open my own training and development consulting firm, Upward Performance.

Why I became an entrepreneur:

I became an entrepreneur because I always had a burning desire to be in business for myself, to help others and showcase my passion. I knew God had blessed me with the unique ability to intuitively connect with people and inspire them to act and manifest their highest potential. Also, it is awesome to pay it forward. I did not just arrive and become who I am today. I had life lessons and people take a chance on me. I have been blessed with mentors that invested their time by giving me feedback and challenging assignments in the effort of seeing me evolve professionally. That process in itself is what grew my passion to see others succeed. I also wanted to provide guidance for clients in order to make their growth and development easier.

Unfortunately, I had to chase my opportunities to be mentored; initially I was ignored and brushed off. The sad truth is that some people do not see the potential in you so you are discarded and not taken seriously. It was an uphill battle trying to convince people to help me develop. Development shouldn't require begging. That is the driving force behind Upward Performance. With Upward Performance, I work with individual clients or businesses that are seeking to advance their professional development. The ultimate goal is to expand the capabilities of the client and ultimately help them reach their true success.

I became an entrepreneur also because it is imperative that I leave a legacy for my family. I want to have something I can pass down to them. I want to build an empire that will ultimately give me the flexibility to be in control of my schedule and plan my work around important family. Also I have unlimited earning potential and I determine my destiny. Being a mompreneur gives me all of the rewards and challenges to keep me driven and unyielding to defeat.

I have seen so many people live out their dreams and find the gratification I dreamed of. While working for Sam's Club I had an inside look at small business owners manage their business. I have witnessed countless entrepreneurs find ways to reinvent themselves and provide a service and or products that continuously make their business relevant.

I was also intrigued by the Sam's Club concept of a business helping a business. Early in my career I decided to learn as much as possible from the retail giant and strengthen my business acumen. I knew if I took every stretch assignment, volunteered for special assignments and purposely asserted myself in other aspects of the business, I would get a comprehensive insight into running a successful business.

I opened Upward Performance with the same concept in mind; I am helping small businesses and non-profit organizations with employee training and leadership development. I have many years of experience in analyzing, developing, cultivating, mentoring, recruiting and shifting leaders by empowering them to soar into their purpose. In addition working for Walmart Stores Inc. (Walmart Stores and Sam's Clubs), I learned how to be an entrepreneur. I learned how to manage a P&L statement, purchase merchandise, highs and lows leadership, merchandising, marketing, time management, sales and lead multi-unit facilities. This was the best hands on schooling one could dream of. It only makes sense for me to now use these skills to build my dream.

Obstacles I faced as a Mompreneur

An obstacle I have faced becoming a Mompreneur is battling fear. I sometimes flip-flopped with trusting my intuition and running with it. Charting into a new business venture that is not backed by a major corporation and assuming all the risks has been unnerving. I have invested my money and time into a venture that I was unsure if I would reap the benefits. I had a lot of fear behind wondering if I would make it. What if I do not get any business? Will I spend more investing to get my business off the ground than I would see as a return? What will my current employer think of my business venture? Will my family and friends support me? Should I take this risk or play it safe with a well-established company and build a nest egg? Will people take me seriously as a black woman entrepreneur? I pondered, heavily debated, talked myself out of it and mentally disabled my confidence. Fear took over. At the lowest point of self-pity I came across a Bible verse that became a game-changer. After reading this verse I instantly arrested all negative thoughts and cancelled that self-doubt with meditating day and night on Philippians 4:6-7 ESV:

"Do not be anxious about anything, but in everything by prayer and supplication with thanksgiving let your request be made known to God. And the peace of God, which surpasses all understanding, will guard your hearts and your minds in Christ Jesus."

It wasn't until I acted on Faith and saw who I was in Christ that I took the step to secure my purpose. I came to realize that these fears weren't new. I experienced these fears every time I tried something new with my career. I did not always succeed in every career move; however, I did learn something with every experience. I came to the conclusion that the same could be true of this new venture. In the small instance that I did not succeed the way I would like, there would always be something to learn- a takeaway. Having a key takeaway from every experience is rewarding. The experience allows growth and positions me to do better the next time. Athena Singh said, "never trust your fears they don't know your strength".

Another obstacle I have faced is balancing the responsibilities of work and home. Many refer to the term of life-balance or life-integration. I learned from my corporate job days to not dwell on what I missed. Meaning if I missed a game, community parent teacher meeting or after school function I wasn't going to collapse in pity. Instead I use S.W.O.T. It is common business strategy to use the **SWOT** (strength, weakness, opportunities and threats) method. As I mentioned, many skills used in business I found to be transferable as a mom. The SWOT method can be used personally as well. I learned to make it work!

If there is a special event at times, my husband will go to the event and record what I was miss and I would do the same for him if he had a business to tend to. As a busy mom of three I am sure to check everyone's schedule and my husband and I make it work! At minimum, we ensure that at least one of us is present at our children's events. This is a priority for I know firsthand what it feels like not to have parents present at games or recitals. Growing up it made me feel hurt and sometimes neglected. It wasn't until I matured and became a busy mother that I was able to understand and see it from a different perspective. Regardless of whether I am there or not, I do ensure my children know I am incredibly proud of their participation in extracurricular activities. I do this by being present as often as I can. I collect memories by taking pictures, capturing video, sharing on social media, practicing with them (yes... as a wrestling mom, I learned the wrestling moves, I knew the all cheers as a cheer mom and I know how to tumble for my baby gymnast) and providing them with positive affirmations.

Being in corporate America at times I travelled intensively. In my early years of business traveling, I had a hard time coping with being separated from my children for multiple days at a time. I felt as if I was neglecting them and wasn't living up to my motherly duties of seeing them daily and tending to their needs. Unfortunately travelling was a non-negotiable with my employer. My living situation depended on a dual income; so I had to do what I had to do whether I liked it or not.

I later was able to overcome the separation anxiety and realized that I was ultimately doing what was best for my family. Now when I travel we have found ways to stay connected while away. Nowadays with technology, it has help to lessen the mommy guilt. Using Messenger or FaceTime is a great way to stay connected and see my children while I am away. It's always ideal to hold them too, but to have real time visual connectivity is awesome while away on business. I have my children take a picture of their homework and send it to me via text or e-mail. I review their homework and coach them on their studies as needed. In addition, the school uploads their assignments on the school website and I have visibility to see when they have missing assignments and how they are performing. I have remote access to intervene as needed.

Parent Teacher conferences can be done remotely if I am away on business. I can conference using a webinar or phone conference. All documents that are to be viewed can be done using technology. I learned if there is a will, there is a way. I was able to fill the void of missing out by using innovative methods to stay connected.

Enlisting support was another obstacle. I knew from working with a retail giant that I wasn't going too far without the support of others. I needed a tribe. I needed to trust my instincts and trust people to help me build a tribe. Collaborative minds are essential for business growth, development and maintaining a competitive edge. Helen Keller said "Alone we can do so little; together we can do so much". I have learned the market is large enough for liked minds to work together to improve and grow our businesses versus competing and limiting the possibility greatness. I used these three methods to build a trusting tribe:

First, I networked with other entrepreneurs and exchanged best practices and ideas. Some of the ideas I was able to use was to use virtual assistants, researchers, collaborate on projects jointly with other entrepreneurs, schedule feedback sessions with clients to gain insights on how to enhance the experience, pilot new rollouts before global execution and staying flexible in tweaking the business to remain competitive in the market. I also obtained referrals of people they have used or know of that offered services that I needed for my business. Second, I became a recruiter of my inner circle and found individuals that possessed the knowledge; skills and abilities needed to fill my business needs. I came to realize I can't run and grow my business alone. I knew success wouldn't come as a loner. I am fond of what Mae Jemison said, "Never limit yourself because of others' limited imagination; never limit others because of your own limited imagination."

Thirdly, I built a connection with my followers. Using continuous updates on social media and actively engaging with the followers gave Upward Performance a boost in credibility. In doing this I have created a tribe that became the word of mouth marketing team. I needed massive endorsements and the followers of my brand in order to increase business. This reminds me of a quote by Scott Cook "a brand is no longer what we tell the customer it is- it is what the customers tell each other it is".

Accepting rejection was something I also learned to embrace. Of course it is not easy receiving rejections such as I am not interested; we will go with someone else; or we are looking for a company with a larger client base. It was already difficult enough for me as an introvert to muster the courage and boldness to ask for the sale. Getting rejected was something I wasn't accustomed to.

I must be honest; the first few declines were detrimental to my self-esteem and halted my business. I took the rejection as I wasn't prepared for nor worthy of their business. All of the fears I thought that I conquered came back in my mind and tormented me. I found myself having a pity party; it wasn't a good feeling.

I recognized that the thoughts were detrimental. Therefore, I decided to bounce back and refocus. Self-pity hinders growth and productivity. I knew I couldn't live like that. I decided to ignite my inner strength and turn my results around. I realized that I must promote my business and sell the services that I provide. A part of selling is knowing how to move past the rejection and bounce to the next prospect without skipping a beat! I used some of my experience from corporate America, specifically not focusing on what I wasn't getting, but what I could gain if I kept asking. Continuous improvement and persistence is the golden nugget for success. I know now that I can't avoid hearing "no". It is imperative to understand why the sale was declined. Getting insight on the opposition helps me build a better sales pitch. In addition, I should be prepared for a no response and have a rebuttal waiting. These are tips for having an effective closing strategy.

Realizing my worth was a hurdle. I found myself offering services for free quite often and I wasn't confident in my pricing. I soon realized every time I reduced my fees I devalued my product and appeared desperate for a sale. I recalled my retail management concepts and put them into action. Sometimes all that is needed is a marketing strategy to gain clients and get them to your site or place of business. I wasn't doing that. I was heavily discounting just to get business. I learned to market my business and attract new clients by offering sample sizes of the services I offer. I learned to use techniques to generate sales leads such as discounting a product as a newer version is coming out. Keeping the peak time of the business in mind, I would offer incredible deals. For example, many businesses offer holiday pricing for many services or merchandise.

I also learned how use my competitors to my advantage. I would study my competition and focus on what they were doing well. It is easy to point out flaws, but it takes a special mind to see what is working and how I can retool my business to yield a positive result and have a competitive edge.

I also had to overcome my fear of trusting others. I started out with everything being a big secret and not wanting to connect with others because of fear that my ideas would be stolen. My fears may have had some validity, but I refused to major in the minor possibilities. I thought of a quote from Helen Keller "alone we can do so little; together we can do so much". This quote was just in time to ignite my inner passion to make it happen. I decided to step out on faith and at my surprise collaborating with other mompreneurs has been the most rewarding experience. I found early on that trading best practices and working in teams is great for development and networking. It is enough business for us mompreneurs to operate and run separate successful businesses; we can grow personally and professionally together. In addition, we can build a great rapport with other like-minded mompreneurs. There is so much value in elevating each other. Paul Solarz said it best *"collaboration allows us to know more than we are capable of knowing by ourselves"*.

Entrepreneurship makes me a better mother:

I say this because I am continuously evolving into a better business leader. Many of the traits of a business leader are transferable skills that can be easily applied in parenting. Some of the challenges I faced as a mother and also as a business leader have been eye-opening. For one, I had difficulties with saying no to my children sometimes. Considering I do travel a lot I may over compensate by giving them everything they ask for to make up for being gone. I had to shift that mindset and ensure that my children understood hard work pays off. I needed to create a balance. I should not have guilt for being a provider. Therefore, I created conditions so they gained the concept of being rewarded verses asking and receiving every time.

The ability to say no has also provided opportunities in my professional life too. I have struggled for years with taking on more than I should. Being a mompreneur has taught me that my time is very valuable and the time I reserve for my family is vital. Mandy Hale said "too busy is a myth. People make time for the things that are really important to them". I have learned to value and manage my time more efficiently. I decided to pick one philanthropy project that will give back to the community verses dabbling in many non-profit organizations. Committing myself to various projects was causing me to spread myself too thin. It wasn't benefiting me as a person nor as a mother. I learned not to deflate myself trying to appease everyone; especially those to whom I am not emotionally invested. My priority was to protect and take care of home and my family. It is vitally important for my children to see me divide my time wisely. Being that my family is my heartbeat, I made sure my time spent with them reflects the effort. I now choose organizations that we all can support as a family. I am teaching my children about giving back to community and serving others and spending time with them simultaneously. We have a lot of wonderful memories serving others with a cheerful heart.

I have definitely had my challenges as a mompreneur. However, dedication has proven to be the key in opening and operating my business. At times, it has felt like a money pit absorbing more than I intended to payout. However, the unwavering desire and passion to see this business successful overshadowed any setbacks or hurdles. This journey has taught me that any form of failure is nothing more than a necessity to transform into greatness. My resilience to failure created an unshakable sense of passion.

Through this journey I have also learned just how important it is to maintain boundaries. I have found I will sometimes make myself available 24/7. This behavior impedes upon my family life. Having a time dedicated to relax and be with my family is mandatory. I soon came to realize that my time is expensive and I can't get time back, but I can strategize to get more money. A part of my drive is staying dedicated without over doing it. Too much of anything is not good for you as a person or the business. I keep myself elevated with powerful quotes such as *"self-discipline isn't just something that happens once and you're done it's a practice"* by Emily Thompson. This quote resonated with me because I needed an effective roadmap for structure. I also needed to institute a process to review correction of errors. My lessons not overdoing myself but yet remaining dedicated to the business need is balance. As a mother, it is important my children know how to appropriate time spent on their passion and still leave time for leisure.

Just as I want my children to understand the importance of that balance, I also want them to see the importance of resilience. I refused to showcase to my children what defeat look like. I refused for them to see how fear can keep a dreamer dreaming and never see the dream flourish. Instead I became a mom who became full of passion. I am deeply inspired by Winston Churchill's statement "Success is the ability to go from one failure to another with no loss of enthusiasm". This quote moved and molded me into a better mompreneur because I did not allow the fears to manifest and block my path to success. Moving along after what is deemed by some as a failure requires true dedication; nothing is more important than dedication. Dedication to my corporate job was a given. I owed it to myself to exhibit the same tenacity in my business venture as well. Quitting is not an option. Having that type of tenacity is modeling proper life skills for my children to follow.

Becoming a Mompreneur is worth it all!

Establishing my business gave me a sense of accomplishment. There are many things I wanted to carry out for myself and my children. I wanted my children to see me evolve from dreamer to doer. It is important my confidence remained high and my family witnessed this. Creating and running my business is a blueprint for my children to follow as they mature and start their own careers. I am leaving a legacy. I am creating a chapter in my book of life. I am living in the moment and not taking for granted how I turned a daydream into a reality. My children and husband motivate me to keep pushing. I decided I will succeed because I can. Nothing else mattered. The noise of fear, naysayers, jealousy and incompetence were properly placed away from me and that is where freedom interceded. My children Alec, Jayla and Kya are my greatest accomplishments and they fuel my perseverance and passion as a mompreneur!

ABOUT THE AUTHOR

HR Professional & Motivational Speaker

Jennifer Logan, founder and owner of Upward Performance, graduated from the Anthem University with a BS in Human Resources on 2016. She is a talented HR professional with over 20 years of experience. She has worked with major retailers across the U.S. and is also a certified speaker and trainer of the John Maxwell Team. As an HR professional, Jennifer is a skilled analyzer. She analyzes the emerging needs of staff members to offer solutions for organizational success. Working as a Market Human Resource Manager at Walmart Stores Inc., Sam's Club Division, she has covered many states including PA, NJ, MD, NY, and CT. She is currently supporting the Sam's Clubs in VA and WV.

Born in Virginia, Jennifer is married to Etienne with three children Alec, Jayla, and Kya. Motivational speaker by interest, Jennifer has years of experience in speaking in conferences. Every organization that she has been a part of, she speaks on motivational topics to benefit organizations.

As a dynamic speaker, she is an expert at topics related to leadership, achieving goals, being selfless, personal development, being purposeful, staying encouraged, and more. Jennifer also excels in writing books and is a future bestselling author of Ignite: Pushing Yourself Outside of your Comfort Zone. Ignite will be released in June of 2017.

She actively blogs about leadership topics and motivates many individuals as possible. She has extensive experience in grooming leaders to perform their tasks much more professionally. With her skills and expertise, Jennifer designs strategic and individualized plans to help professionals excel in their career.

Jennifer also actively hosts biweekly webinars and mastermind classes for professionals. These webinars provide professionals sound advice on leadership development. Jennifer has a vast experience in handling HR needs of retail giants like Target, Lowe's and Sam's Club and Walmart. She has the skills and ability to help reduce organizational risk by addressing employee performance. With her wise words and extensive experience, she is able to handle even the most crucial employee engagement. Having such high level expertise in HR, leadership and motivational speaking gives her the ability to form performance driven teams. As a result, Jennifer founded the company Upward Performance to expand the client in maximizing their potential for the business realm.

www.upwardperformance.com
Facebook.com/Upward Performance

Chapter Twelve

A Mom By God's Loving Grace
By: Trinese Summerlin

How it all began

No morning sickness, no uncomfortable pregnancy, no long intense labor pains, no hospital stay...but I suddenly became a mother. You see, I did not give birth to any children of my own, but God placed several children in my life that I call my own. I must say that they all have been the best gift that I have ever received. Being an entrepreneur came a little after motherhood and it was just as exciting. It's amazing how things happen in your life that you can't explain; you just kind of go with the flow hoping that everything will work out. Everything that has been placed in my life since October of 1998 was just like that; however I now know it was all part of God's divine plan for me. My marriage, my divorce, becoming a step-mom, raising my nephews, opening my businesses, as well as all the trials and tribulations and wonderful opportunities that He blessed me with- it all happened the way that it should have.

Single Life to Step-Mom

My step-children were almost teenagers when I got married. And let me tell you, they gave me a run for my money! But the greatest reward was being able to build relationships with each and every one of them. Now, many years later, they feel as if I made a difference in their lives, but the truth is that they made one in mine. Although I knew what books said on how to care for children, I never really had to care for any on my own. And there was no manual that was delivered with these teenagers when they came over to visit (lol). They threw parties in the house while we were gone, stayed on the phone late on school nights, would sneak in my room to wear my makeup and clothes, and any other crazy thing a teenager would do to drive a parent absolutely insane. This was all very new to me and I must say that I handled it quite well. I was able to build a new small business while building relationships with my new children. The challenge wasn't getting to know them; it was the long hours that I spent building my business. Becoming a step-mom was my first shot at motherhood and I thank God for the opportunity.

The Marriage, the Divorce, and then after the Divorce
Marriage

Most people are shocked when I say this, but I never wanted to get married. I was content with my single life until I met this guy that I fell in love with and wanted to marry. He gave me this family that was new and different for me and I would like to say that the love we shared was unconditional. This marriage gave me the opportunity to learn how to be a mom, a wife, and most of all figure out the balance. What do I mean when I say the "balance"? The balance of trying to determine how to divide yourself between the two things that you love so deeply, the love of your family and the love of your business. How do you make everyone happy and still be successful or even survive? My answer to the question is prayer, support, and communication. Although my marriage did not work out, I can definitely say I prayed a lot and tried to communicate as much as I could. The one thing that a married entrepreneur needs is support. Without it the relationship may become challenging.

The Divorce

In my opinion going through a divorce is worse than losing a loved one to death. The challenges and emotional stress that I experienced while going through this difficult event in my life kept me in prayer. But it also made me appreciate the blessings that were given to me. Blessings such as amazing stepchildren and a thriving business. I remember in the past feeling that if my business failed that I would just start over; it wouldn't be a big deal. It wasn't until the imminent threat of losing my business that I realized how much it meant to me. You see, this divorce did something to me. It gave me courage and strength. I wasn't ready to give up something that I knew that God had blessed me with. I continued to pray and God saw me through one of the most difficult times of my life.

Although my marriage ended, I am blessed to still have a friendship with my ex-husband. I also still have those beautiful relationships my stepchildren- the children that gave me my first shot at being a mom. I love them ALL!

After the Divorce

After my divorce I spent a lot of time working and getting to know myself again. I spent time figuring out what really made me happy. When you are moving rapidly on a daily basis, you don't stop to think about the things that bring you happiness. So, I spent the next couple of years trying to determine what ultimately bring me peace and happiness. I moved, decided to hire a personal trainer, took charge of my health, went to graduate school to complete my Master's degree, traveled to visit my friends, went back to my alma mater a couple times in one year, decreased my work week to 5 days instead of 7, spent time with my family, and most importantly, I did exactly what I wanted to do. I realized that I was in charge and that I was in control of my destiny. I choose ME!

Then came the hidden blessing from God; the blessing that saved my life. A blessing that I was not expecting at ALL! It was a blessing that continues to greet me with a smile every day. God gave me the opportunity to honor my sister's last wish. October of 1998 is when it all began. I can remember this day like it was yesterday. I was sitting at the table in my sister's kitchen when she asked the life- changing question. She said, "Nese, (that is the nickname that my family gave me) if anything were to happen to me would you take care of my children?" Now of course I said yes. At that moment I never imagined that shortly thereafter my sister and her children would be involved in a tragic car accident. The children survived the accident, but my sister was taken away from me forever.

I got the opportunity to fulfill her last wish, I got my opportunity to give motherhood a second shot, I got my opportunity to make a difference in my nephews' lives. I was SUPER excited! Raising them was something that I wanted to do immediately after their mother's death, but life's circumstances didn't give me the immediate opportunity.

When my two nephews finally came to live with me they were so much older and had been through so much. After listening to some of the stories that they shared with me, I could diagnose them with so many things. But the diagnosis that I gave them was "a lack of a Mother's love". They were dealing with so many different emotions. The life events that took place in those previous years had left them internally bruised. The younger nephew had a speech impairment. His stuttering was so severe that sometimes it took 30 seconds before he could speak one word. He also struggled with confidence, trust, and faith. He was very negative and didn't believe in himself nor anything or anyone else for that matter. He would often say, "why try because something bad is just going to happen". But you know that God delivered him, right? Let me tell you this- after being with him six months, the stuttering went away. Yup, just like that he stopped stuttering. One day I was talking with his older brother and I said, "did you notice that your brother doesn't stutter anymore?" He was like, "yea, I did notice that!" Then we began to discuss how good God is and talked about His many blessings. We did that often in my house. We would just converse and share old memories, laugh, and talk about how amazing God is.

Now that was just the beginning of his time with me. Since the beginning, he has experienced many not so great things, and God has delivered him from it all. He no longer thinks negatively. He shares with me what he would like his future to look like. Now he has so much confidence about himself that I have to knock him down a couple of notches every now and then. He also has faith which allows him to take the steps to leading a successful life. I call him "my Saving Grace". You should hear him at times encouraging me and giving me advice. It puts a smile on my face and after my divorce that is exactly what I needed.

Now let's talk about the older nephew and how he tried to give me a heart attack! When we reconnected it took a little longer to reach him. He really struggled with trust, self-confidence and lacked the ability to allow himself to love others. So instead of showing love he expressed anger through his actions and behavior;

not only to himself, but also to others. He tried to push everyone away and it hurt me tremendously. It hurt because I felt his pain and I understood his struggle. But most of all it hurt because I could not take it away. He was the child that had the closest relationship with his mother. He was also the child that remembers everything about the accident and the death of his mother. Right after the car wreck he was the one that got out of the car to get help. He remembers the nine days that his mother survived in the hospital; the last nine days of her life. He also remembers not being able to see her again until the funeral. So you see, his pain went untreated for several years until he was given the opportunity to heal.

Although his behaviors would cause him and others grief, I still had a way to get him to connect to the process of healing. It took him some time to realize that love doesn't mean pain, but eventually God did deliver him. The one thing that allowed me to connect with him and to help him heal was the relationship that I had built with him when he was a child, years before his mother even passed away. He was the eldest grandchild, great-grandchild, and nephew. He received extra attention from not only me, but the entire family which enabled relationships and bonds to be created at a very young age. Thankfully he held onto the memories and feelings until we were able to reconnect again.

God's love and grace saved him from himself, because believe me the struggle was real. When I look at him now and I see what he has overcome it brings tears to my eyes. I say to myself at times, "I am so glad that God loves him"; he is such a beautiful person. When he allowed himself to love, when he allowed himself to trust, and when he built confidence and gained faith, God delivered him and his life began to change.

As I share these stories about my nephews, who are now 23 and 26, I smile. I smile because God gave me an opportunity to be a mother- not once, but twice. Although I am a stepmother it is different because my stepchildren actually have a mom that is alive so my motherly duties were limited and came with boundaries. My nephews had ME and no one else to be a "mother"; I did not have limits and boundaries. Best of all I also have them, which means that we have each other. That, brings me JOY!

I can honestly say that even though I received custody of them at a much later time in their lives, I am the one that raised them. Although I did not give birth to any children, I understand and feel the connection that a mother has with her child. Because I experienced those moments when I wanted to blow up a school or shoot a teacher because of something that happened with my boys, because I have wanted to hold them until their tummy didn't hurt anymore, because I experienced the necessity of having to punish them because they broke the rules, because I have broken up sibling fights because they both thought they were right, because I have loved them unconditionally, because of these things I am their mother. And for that I will always be grateful.

My Entrepreneur Journey

Let me just start by saying, "I absolutely LOVE what I do"! I would like to call myself a **Child Care Guru.** I started my career in teaching. I was an Early Childhood Educator for five years before moving into the Mental Health Field. I worked with children with challenging behaviors helping them maintain normal behaviors in a typical classroom environment. You know, the kids that might throw a chair, bite their friends, knock over a shelf or table, or run out of the classroom- I worked with them. I would help faculty to develop a plan to keep these children in the classroom. I worked in the Mental Health Industry for five years before having the opportunity to purchase a child care center.

I learned about the opportunity to purchase my Center through one of the Child Care Owners that I was working with. She told me that she was going to close the Center because she had just had an inspection from the state and there were too many things that needed attention. I immediately became interested! After the death of my sister and after my divorce, fear was something that I did not feel. I went from being this shy and quiet person to a fearless and bold individual that conquered some of the dreams that previously I just carried around in my mental journal. I was happy that I had taken charge of my life and that I learned that tomorrow is definitely not promised to anyone. I let her know that I was interested and I went on a journey to find the finances to purchase this business from her.

Now I thought that this was going to be an easy process. I thought that I could just walk into a bank and they would give me money,. NOT; that did not happen! I tried to get a second mortgage on property, I tried to go back to school so that I could get the loan money, I did everything that I thought was necessary. But then it dawned on me- I hadn't asked God for this business. I had forgotten to pray! I felt like giving up, but in that moment of despair I had a talk with God. I asked him to work it out for me. No matter what the outcome I knew that it would be of Him and I was ok with that. After my talk with the Man from above, I called the owner and told her that I wasn't able to come up with the money for the business. Let me tell you that God is SO AMAZING! Do you know that He worked it out for me! She heard me out, and then she began to tell me what special arrangement that should would work out with me. She told me that if I put down $7500, I could make monthly payments until the loan was paid in full. You want to talk about someone being excited; I was OVERJOYED! You know I had to do my happy dance!!! In order to make my dream come true I had to ask my family. What a blessing that they had no problem with investing in me. [I would love to expose them individually in this book, but I'm not sure how they would feel about it. If anyone of you are reading this, I truly thank you for believing in me. I am so grateful to have each and every on of you in my life!] The moment that I made that silent prayer to myself, and decided to give up on my dream, things worked themselves out and I am forever grateful!

The Business

The business that I was blessed with is a Child Development Center/Preschool. I incorporated my business in November of 2003 and became a licensed Center on February 23, 2004. I was a Business Owner- a real entrepreneur! I could not believe it! I was so excited I didn't know what to do! Once I received the keys to the business and received the approval from the State of Ohio, I began conducting business. Now the crazy part is that I hadn't run a business before; however I am happy that I had the new fearless attitude!. I didn't do my normal routine of writing everything out and over analyzing; I just DID IT! I didn't let anything get in my way. Throughout all of the trials and tribulations, bad business decisions, and financial insecurities, I just keep pushing forward. For the first time in my life I had gained tons of courage and I had no fear.

I worked sun up to sundown getting things the way that I wanted them. I didn't sleep much, I didn't spend much time with my family, I just followed my vision. I was just living out my dream and it felt good. When people would see me in my hustle flow, they would think that I had been in business for decades. When I told them that I had just purchased the business they would tell me how easy I made owning a business look.

During the second year of my business I was able to hire a receptionist. She worked for me two months before she put in her two-week notice. When I wished her well and told her that if she ever needed anything to call me, she responded by saying that she was leaving because she was going to go and open a restaurant. Although I was shocked, I was very encouraging. I did not judge her for I knew how much God could bless anyone. Ironically she called me a month later asking for her job back. She told me that things were very expensive and it was much harder than she anticipated. She also shared with me that she thought that she could pull it off because I did it. She said to me, "I just knew that if you could do it, so could I. We are about the same age so I figured that I could just start something and live out my dream of owning a business too." She said that I made it look so easy, so she figured that she would give it a try. Now I held all of my emotions inside (lol), I remained professional and then I told her this, "Just because things did not work out right now doesn't mean that they will not work out later. Maybe it was just bad timing. But the next time that you go after your dream, make sure that you are doing it for all of the right reasons. I will even help you with the initial business steps".

After hearing several times from individuals that I made owning a business look so easy and after receiving several phone calls from people asking me how to start a daycare business, I knew that this was definitely what I was called to do. I find joy and pleasure in working with children as well as helping others to succeed. I have been in the early childhood industry since 1994, and within the time, I have coached hundreds of Early Childhood Educators on professionalism, successful classroom arrangement, building social emotional awareness in the classroom and educational growth.

The name of my business is Inspired By You Child Development Center. As I shared earlier, the death of my sister inspired me to live for today. So the name is Inspired by You is a message to my sister. The business was a blessing from God, so the inspiration from both my sister and God gave me the name.

The Balance

Let's face it, most entrepreneurs struggle with balancing their family, work and the business. But like I mentioned earlier, I figured out balance while being married. I learned that the secret of balance is figuring out what works for everyone involved, so communication is key. Balance is not going to be the same for everyone; you have to figure out what balance means for you and your loved ones. Once you figure it out, BAM! Implement and execute.

Now I didn't say that balance wouldn't be challenging. When my nephews first came to live with me, I was in that space of "Doing Me" and finding "Peace and Happiness". The thought of having two young adolescent boys with me did not scare me, because I knew that together we could all figure it out. But I have to be honest, it did change the way that I thought and did things. What I learned was that it was no longer just ME. I had two young men that trusted and depended on me. So, my choices and decisions about a lot of things became about them and how it would affect them. I had to sacrifice some freedom. But I didn't mind; I enjoyed being around them. They brought me peace and happiness, and that was what I set out to accomplish when I went on the journey "To Do Me". We all traveled together and took this thing called LIFE head on! We built relationships, memories, and most all a bond that no one can take away from us.

As life's circumstance caused roadblocks which forced us to make sacrifices, we created our own family. We began to trust one another and to depend on each other's presence which allowed us to feel more safe and secure, emotionally stable, and supported.

We began to be there for one another and that felt good. So our roadblocks and sacrifices made us stronger! People say to me all of the time, "that was nice of you to take in your sister's kids", "that was very unselfish of you", "they are really blessed to have someone like you in their life" or on the flip side of things, they say things like, "she doesn't have any children, she doesn't know what she is doing", but guess what, I DON'T CARE! And to be quite honest I never did! I am just being the person that God has created me to be, and that is a person that didn't think twice when I became a stepmom nor when my sister asked me to care for her boys. I am someone whose life made a detour because God switched up the plan. I am absolutely ok with having had the opportunity to love these boys (I mean young men) unconditionally, and better yet getting the opportunity to be *A Mom by God's Loving Grace!*

ABOUT THE AUTHOR

G. Trinese Summerlin is an Early Childhood Specialist and Child Care Guru. She specializes in working hands on with childcare business owners to open and expand their childcare dreams. Her 20 plus years of experience in the Early Childhood field gives her the expertise to help new business owners. She provides high-level professional training, coaching, and mentoring for individuals that would like to reach the highest level of success.

G. Trinese has created several systems and management tools to help new and current childcare owners open and expand their own business within 90 days. These management tools will help childcare business owners with getting on the right path towards fulfilling dreams, hiring the right staff, increasing enrollment, business organization, as well as other programs that will assist with taking their childcare business to the next level.

G. Trinese is the owner of Inspired By You Child Development Center as well as the founder and CEO of Inspired to Own a Daycare and Inspired to Own a Daycare Boot Camp.

Chapter Thirteen

Making the Case for Successful Moms to Be
By: Tiffany Simmons, Esq.

So you want to run you successful business and successfully manage having a family? Yes you read it, now let's speak into existence that YOUR business is successful and that YOUR family is successful. Well you CAN run your successful business all while enjoying the blessing of being a mother. As a serial entrepreneur I've had my share of success in business. However, my road to motherhood hasn't officially started, but I do have a story to share for those who want to balance making millions while being a mommy. In November 2016, I celebrated seven years as an Attorney and owner of Simmons Law, LLC. Simmons Law is a civil and criminal litigation firm based in Atlanta, GA. I specialize in the areas of business, criminal defense, and entertainment law and I love what I do. I am made for this! When I walk into a courtroom or in any room, my presence is known and felt.

As a licensed attorney I have many career options and a lot of flexibility. I could have easily worked hard to become a Partner at a large firm, or I could have selected to work for a private business as General Counsel. Perhaps I may have even become a District Attorney and worked for the State of Georgia. But as I look back, I know that my path was set for me. Becoming an entrepreneur wasn't a choice; it is a part of my DNA, my makeup, and my destiny.

I come from a rich history of self-made entrepreneurs all who worked hard and blazed their own trail. For instance, I learned that my great grandfather, Taylor, was the first black coffin maker in the State of Michigan. I also learned that my great grandmother helped him in the business as a seamstress for the inside of the coffins. My grandmother, Irene, owned successful hair salons even before completing her high school education as a 4o something year old woman. In Muskegon, MI, my granddad Simmons owned a grocery store that he kept for many years until his children didn't want to help to keep the business running (well that's what I was told by family).

The entrepreneurship "bug" jumped from my elders, to my mom, to me, and other relatives. As a fifth grader I wrote in my very own autobiography that I would be a successful attorney. As a teenager, I started my first business in Grand Rapids, MI. As I think back on my fifth grade autobiography I never talked about "kids, dogs, and a white picket fence", but I had to be thinking of it because I mentioned being successful and success includes family.

Business is what I know and love. Helping people is what I love. Speaking for the voiceless is what I do inside and outside of the courthouse. Simmons Law is one of my business ventures that actually succeeded. Being a serial entrepreneur I've had my share of business "failures". I refer to them instead as learning lessons, because you don't fail unless you quit. One thing I do know is that I will never give up on my heart's desires! Some call it a hustler's spirit, but it is just a natural way of life for me. I always knew my name meant something and I wanted to see it as the owner of many businesses and brands. Since I was a kid I always said that I would create my own legacy for the Simmons name.

Now it's ironic that I'm sharing my story and that I speak of legacy but you haven't heard about my children yet. Well that's because I haven't adopted nor been pregnant....yet! I haven't at any point chosen abortion, nor have I experienced the misfortune or pain of a miscarriage. As a teen my motto was to focus on making something of myself before having kids, which was my plan that I stuck too. Coming from teenage parents my sense of family and desire for kids was different. To be honest, I saw my mom work so hard I vowed that I would become something. I would not live "pay check to pay check." Years later my godmom reminded me that I was that girl in the neighborhood always saying "Nope I won't have no baby on my hip, I'm going away to school." She said I kept my word on that one promise.

But now as a woman who has experienced a marriage, I naturally assumed babies would come with my then husband, but they didn't. I guess since we didn't stay together it is best that we did not get pregnant. The lack of kids in my previous marriage did leave me with questions. I questioned what does success really mean if I am a "successful" lawyer, but I don't come home to a family? Is the sacrifice I've made as an entrepreneur worth me not experiencing motherhood? No! So as much confidence and drive that I possess to have success in my career, I needed to use that same confidence and drive as it relates to success in love and becoming a mother.

The day I talked to Lenise Williams about co-authoring this book, was the day I found out that one of my baby cousins was pregnant. This was the second baby cousin that year that was blessed with pregnancy. This is the same day that I cried real tears. I cried big crocodile tears because I wanted to meet my own little ones. Yes I've had dreams, visions, and thoughts about my unborn kids. My legacy, my twins. Yes I have the names already: initials for both a boy and a girl are CAMP, and yes a long name but a new legacy created through he and I. "He" is the guy that I know that my whole life was prepared for. Not to say that he's perfect, and nor do I believe the fake fairy tale of a knight in shining armor. But he's just perfect for me. Just like Beyoncé says "who wants that perfect love story anyway?" Nah I don't, I just want real love. The type of woman that I am, the type of business owner that I am, and the type of mother that I will be, God has prepared the mate that is for me. I believe in destiny. I believe in meant to be, it's all or nothing! Passionate, real love instead of just "comfortable" love is the goal for my next committed relationship. My future children will experience family from the rules that we create not what I was always taught or what was passed down as tradition. Recently I wrote a poem about family. It reads:

Family: A Poem by Tiffany M. Simmons

What is it? How do you create it? It doesn't just happen when babies are born? It doesn't just happen when the woman holds on despite knowing in her heart it's over. Family isn't created because the guy won't leave out of fear she won't let him see his baby girl. Is family created out of traditions we are taught? Is family shaped by life's challenges? Maybe family is created from unconditional love? Unwavering commitment to a legacy? Family is created when you look at the beauty of life with others.

So can a girl have a family and a career? Definitely! I have and will do it. I will continue to have a thriving career as a lawyer and entertainment mogul and I will have a family. I always said I will not be the rich woman without a family.

Pregnant or Nah? Easier Said Than Done

As a future "mompreneur" I face the obstacle of work /life balance. In my busy career of fixing people's problems or guiding someone's business, maintaining enough balance to be "sane" in my career is a must! The law can be draining, and it's often said that the law is a "jealous mistress." Yes my "law mistress" was extremely jealous. I give my blood, sweat, tears, and money to Simmons Law and the communities we serve. I put a lot of effort on work without experiencing the joys and challenges of raising children. As the saying goes, "If I don't work, I don't eat." But if I want to experience parenthood, I have to put some effort in my personal life. I have to continue loving me first; so that I can be a better *lover* to my mate, and so that I can give my children healthy love. I have to put more effort into meeting new people outside of business. I have to continue to invest in meaningful relationships, and continuing to experience different things. Through putting effort in things that are meaningful outside of career success, I will continue to open the door for love and the opportunity to do what God said do, "be fruitful and multiply."

For instance, when I'm representing a client facing a criminal case, I connect with their families throughout the case. I may meet the client's kids during a court hearing. I may meet a young client's mom and dad while preparing for trial. This connection with the family often leaves me to question my ideas and beliefs on a family. When a person is in crisis situation, as a person dealing with the justice system may feel, you often see who's really "family." To represent a husband who was charged with domestic violence with the child at the home, or to represent a woman who wanted to change a child's last name to her new spouse from the biological dad's name, I've often thought of the effect that these types of situations have on the children. Moreover, I think of how I would behave if I were a parent in these situations. These complex legal issues that surrounds all families and the layers of what happen when two people, ideally in love, create a new life. My experiences with clients either leave me yearning for a family of my own when I see the strength and bond in a family unit, or my client's family dysfunction has left me running away stating "I'm not ready for that!" One thing I can say is that working with people, dealing with their problems, secrets, and family issues has given me a wealth of knowledge to remember for my own family.

As an attorney I don't prefer custody cases and/or divorces. That's really funny that I say that because my very first client in 2009 was a divorce case, and when I was a kid I said I would become a "very successful divorce attorney." In my experience with divorce clients, all logic and common sense is out the window. All you see are people fighting with their emotions. I've seen mothers take action out of spite against dads, and I've seen dads so bitter from the break- up that they don't have the emotional strength, nor the financial resources needed to fight for their rights.

Another obstacle a future mompreneur faces is the perception of "successful women with no children." Oftentimes it's assumed that I don't want kids, or that I selected my career/business over kids. In fact, I do want and I will have children. In my former marriage we tried to get pregnant, especially when I wasn't on birth control for many years, even to this day I don't take birth control due to my concerns on the long- term effects. We tried, but there was never a confirmation that a piece of us was coming into the world. I can't recall too many memories of the disappointment of not getting pregnant and maybe that's a great thing, but nevertheless it didn't happen then. But my time is coming, until then I will keep living.

As an attorney often dealing with high profile cases I deal with a lot of stress, which affects me physically, mentally, and emotionally. Just think about it, I am fixing someone's big problem which could make them money, keep them out of jail, or keep them from paying in a lawsuit. The stakes are high every day in my life and it becomes a tremendous amount of pressure on me! I've been told by doctors that the high stress level may have contributed to my pregnancy challenges. With that said, over the last few years I've actively found ways to reduce my stress level, by committing to a healthy lifestyle. I pray, spend time with God, meditate, workout, travel, laugh a lot, and drink a lot of water. Although I'm a bossy chick, I have a big heart, and I love giving back to the community and to kids. Honestly, I live a blessed life, so it's only right that I live "no stress."

My Business "Babies" Will Prepare Me For Motherhood

When I think of motherhood I think of love. I believe that being a mother is an indescribable experience that is life changing. You see a piece of you and another human in another human! And this little human you have created is unique in their own way, but as mom everything you do is for them. Just thinking about it I get chills, because that's love! I love hard, I mean hard. I remember times I would express that I would die for those that I loved, so I can't imagine what I would do for my own babies.

My thoughts of motherhood motivate me to shoot for my dreams and to continue to fight for the desires of my heart. When it is time for children, through Simmons Law, I have created a better foundation of success for them at birth. Through my other business endeavors, my children and their children will have opportunities within their own family.

Being a business owner is similar to birthing babies in the respect that it's something that you create, you nurture, you protect, you invest, and you love. Over the last seven years I've nurtured my business by working tirelessly for goals that sometimes only I could see. I've protected the Simmons Law name and brand by operating in excellence, integrity, and oftentimes doing what's best for the business and clients regardless of my feelings.

I LOVE SIMMONS LAW! The love of my business is what keeps me going when I want to give up. Love of what I do allows me to keep going when I don't feel like the "Top Best Criminal Defense Attorney in the State of Georgia" as I was named last year. All of the experiences I've faced being a serial entrepreneur since my teenage years will prepare me for the road of motherhood, and if it doesn't that's still my story and I'm sticking to it! Without adding humor, I will say this, God will always prepare you for what he puts in front of you. So with that being said, when the time is right I will be ready and prepared to share new experiences with the family that I create.

Timing... I wanted to have babies and family "success" in my time. My journey over the last six years has taught me that everything will happen in God's timing, I just have to keep moving forward and not back. Being a business owner with thriving business ventures, it is important for me to stay motivated and moving forward despite what I see or face. This self-motivation will be a benefit when I travel the road of motherhood. I want my children to live a better life than I did. I know that I will work to provide a safe place for my children to grow into whom God made them to be. Spending time at the local schools I get to practice with the kids every time I volunteer to speak at "Career Day." Or when Simmons Law hosts events in the community to support kids, I get to have fun on the kids' level. Kids only really want love and they are honest; life hasn't jaded them. In my eyes babies are close to God on this earth and we all have to protect, treat, and teach them well. Community and family is part of the Simmons Law mission and when I do have my own family, the mission will grow even more. I say all of this to say, NO! My future kids will not slow me down from success in business. In fact, my future kids will accelerate me because after work is accomplished I want to spend my time investing in loving them. So to the future mompreneur keep growing, keep living, and keep loving yourself. Those babies are coming one day…. until then keep smiling.

Is My Path Worth It?

We all have thoughts on how our life could be different. As for me, I have no regrets about my path to successful entrepreneurship. Nor do I have any regrets of my path as a future mompreneur. Had I not experienced what I've been through in life how would I know what I could endure? How would I know what to teach my children about life? And of course I needed to travel my path to have some wild stories to share with my kids when they become adults.

Practical Tips on Business, Babies, and Balance

- Schedule time to take care of you. Oftentimes mompreneurs put everything first and take care of themselves last. How can you pour into anyone if you are empty?
- Create a schedule. Schedule time for your child that is separate from your business life. You need those real moments to connect with the ones who love you the most. Those moments with family often recharge me when I'm drained from the business. Alternatively, if you can incorporate your kids in your

business do so! I learned how to run a business by watching other family members. Create events to promote your business that is kid friendly, that way you can include your kids in your mompreneur success.

- Build your team, your tribe to support your business and support your children. When you have to fill an order for a client but your kid needs to be picked up, that's when your tribe comes in. Family or friends that you can trust and that you all can support each other while you build your business is a great resource. In addition to those being available to support you, make sure you are available for them. Remember the old saying, "united we stand, divided we fall?"

- Be courageous! You can still reach your goals after having a baby. Sometimes mothers are discouraged because it's hard to imagine balancing entrepreneurship and motherhood. But relax; I've heard from some great moms that their children were their inspiration to succeed in their careers. Either they knew "my kid looked up to me" or "I couldn't fail I had a baby to feed" but whatever the reason, sometimes the maternal instinct puts a woman into overdrive to become successful. You can do it mompreneur!

- Have faith and trust God. As an entrepreneur we walk by faith every day. So when you are a successful mompreneur you should do the same. Have faith that you can handle being a parent and a business owner. Trust God in the times that you a faced with challenges in your home or in your career.

ABOUT THE AUTHOR

Tiffany M. Simmons is an attorney and managing partner at Simmons Law, a law firm in Atlanta, Georgia, which focuses on criminal defense, business law/civil litigation, and entertainment. She represents high profile clients, businesses, and the everyday citizen and is dedicated to being a relentless advocate for her community.

Attorney Simmons has worked on high profile cases such as:
 • Lead counsel for Christopher LeDay, the man arrested on his job after posting the Alton Sterling police shooting video on social media.
 • Co-counsel in the successful secured acquittals in the trial (and multiple re-trials) of Lula Smart and the Quitman 12 (a group of minority political activists unfairly accused of voter fraud in the Brooks County, Georgia election) in 2013.
 • Co-counsel on litigation team for a case that appeared on CNBC's "American Greed", a weekly, true crime television documentary series.

A distinguished leader in her community, Simmons has served as a board member to several organizations with a mission to provide greater access to healthcare and resources for the welfare and education of children. In 2014, Attorney Simmons instituted the "Simmons Law Memorial Scholarship," an academic scholarship for the benefit of students attending college. On Sundays in Atlanta, Tiffany serves dinners to the homeless, provides them with clothes and toiletries. Additionally, Tiffany serves as a Non-Governmental Observer in May, 2016 for the American Bar Association (ABA) at the United States Military Commissions in Guantanamo Bay, Cuba. As a Georgia Delegate for the ABA, Tiffany spoke in support of law enforcement wearing body cameras when interacting with civilians.

Simmons was most recently named by The American Institute of Criminal Law Attorneys the "Top Ten Best Criminal Female Lawyers" in Georgia. Tiffany earned the Martindale-Hubbell Client Distinction Award from 2013-2016 and selected by *Attorney At Law* Magazine "Attorneys to Watch" in 2015. In 2015, she was the recipient of the *Rising in Community Excellenc*e Award (RICE award) for her philanthropic efforts in the community. She is the Co-chair of the Criminal Justice Committee Solo/Small Firm section of the AMA, and currently serves as the 2016-2018 Chair of the Atlanta's John Marshall Law School Alumni Association.

Simmons' likeable personality and passionate advocacy has landed her to be featured on media programs, including CNN's *HLN After Dark*, as well as talk and syndicated radio shows. Simmons is a published author and currently has a new e-book, "Create Your Law Business For This Generation". She is also a speaker, pushing her series, "More Than Just A Pretty Face", to empower women - young and old - to be freed from labels and perspectives that keep them from realizing their dreams.
Law Firm Site: slfirmllc.com

www.ingramcontent.com/pod-product-compliance
Lightning Source LLC
Chambersburg PA
CBHW071417180526
45170CB00001B/138